AUTÉNTICO

AUTÉNTICO

The Definitive Guide to Latino Career Success

SECOND EDITION

Dr. Robert Rodriguez and Andrés T. Tapia

FOREWORD BY HENRY CISNEROS

BK

Berrett–Koehler Publishers, Inc.

Berrett-Koehler Publishers, Inc.
1333 Broadway, Suite 1000
Oakland, CA 94612-1921
Tel: (510) 817-2277
Fax: (510) 817-2278
www.bkconnection.com

ORDERING INFORMATION
Quantity sales. Special discounts are available on quantity purchases by corporations, associations, and others. For details, contact the "Special Sales Department" at the Berrett-Koehler address above.
Individual sales. Berrett-Koehler publications are available through most bookstores. They can also be ordered directly from Berrett-Koehler: Tel: (800) 929-2929; Fax: (802) 864-7626; www.bkconnection.com.
Orders for college textbook / course adoption use. Please contact Berrett-Koehler: Tel: (800) 929-2929; Fax: (802) 864-7626.

Distributed to the U.S. trade and internationally by Penguin Random House Publisher Services.

Berrett-Koehler and the BK logo are registered trademarks of Berrett-Koehler Publishers, Inc.

Printed in the United States of America

Berrett-Koehler books are printed on long-lasting acid-free paper. When it is available, we choose paper that has been manufactured by environmentally responsible processes. These may include using trees grown in sustainable forests, incorporating recycled paper, minimizing chlorine in bleaching, or recycling the energy produced at the paper mill.

Library of Congress Cataloging-in-Publication Data

Names: Rodriguez, Robert, 1969- author. | Tapia, Andrés, 1960- author. |
   Cisneros, Henry, writer of foreword.
Title: Auténtico : the definitive guide to Latino career success / Dr.
   Robert Rodriguez & Andrés T. Tapia ; foreword by Henry Cisneros.
Description: Second edition. | Oakland, CA : Berrett-Koehler Publishers,
   Inc., [2021] | Includes bibliographical references and index.
Identifiers: LCCN 2021005974 | ISBN 9781523093045 (paperback) | ISBN
   9781523093052 (adobe pdf) | ISBN 9781523093069 (epub)
Subjects: LCSH: Hispanic Americans--Employment. | Hispanic American
   executives. | Discrimination in employment--United States.
Classification: LCC HD8081.H7 R633 2021 | DDC 658.4/0908968073--dc23
LC record available at https://lccn.loc.gov/2021005974

Second Edition
27 26 25 24 23 22 21   10 9 8 7 6 5 4 3 2 1

Book design and production: Seventeenth Street Studios
Cover designer: Alvaro Villanueva

"*Se hace camino al andar.*"

You make the path as you walk it.

—Antonio Machado

DEDICATIONS

Andrés:

A mi papá, who was that Latino executive who role-modeled thought leadership, relentlessness, risk-taking, and giving back.

A mi Tío Douglas, who through passionate Sporting Cristal soccer weekends at el Estadio Nacional, shared his love for me.

To Lori, who from the beginning saw and loved the Peruano in me.

A m'hija Marisela quien vive el espíritu Latinx con toda pasión.

Robert:

To Mom and Dad: Thanks for all the sacrifices you made to help give me more opportunity and a better life. This book extends your legacy of always giving back to the community. All my love.

To Bailey and Benjamin: I can have no better ambition in life than to be the best father I can be for you both. Hope you see this book as a gift as it relates to your Latino identity. Love you.

To Sofia: I feel so fortunate to be the subject of your grace and favor. Thank you for helping me connect with my inner Latino self. Te amo.

CONTENTS

FOREWORD

By Henry Cisneros

I n order for our country to be strong and prosperous through the decades of this century, it is imperative that the American Latinos community succeed in every realm of American life. Latinos today are about sixty million people in a nation of 320 million, roughly 19 percent of the U.S. population. By 2050 demographers estimate that Latinos, the fastest-growing segment of the national population, will be about one hundred million people when the nation reaches four hundred million residents, constituting 25 percent of the nation's population. A quick calculation tells us that the increase of forty million Latinos over that time will be one-half of the nation's net addition of eighty million people: that is, Latinos will account for fully half of the nation's total growth.

It is clear that the Latino dynamic will be one of the most important forces shaping the future of the United States. Because the Latino population is on average younger than the national average, those growth numbers mean that in all the critical dimensions of our nation's social and economic advancement— children in school, access to higher education, workforce composition, household formations, consumer spending, home and auto expenditures, and leadership development—Latinos will be an immense force for progress.

Because of the outsize proportion of Latino growth, in virtually every aspect of American well-being, Latinos will move the needle, for better or for worse. The mathematical principles of larger numbers dictate that Latinos will be key determinants of national progress in the most important dimensions of American economic, social, and educational attainment. In short, American progress will depend in great measure on American Latino progress.

As at every point in American history and as with every emergent group in American society, Latino progress will be driven by improvements in Latino economic well-being based on steady increases in income and wealth. There are many levers to accelerate incomes and wealth:

- Investments in human capital through education and training
- Small business formations
- Wage and earnings increases
- Advances in net worth and ownership levels
- Participation in retirement and pension plans
- Career advancement in corporate structures

Dr. Robert Rodriguez and Andrés Tapia have updated *Auténtico*, a book that integrates all these elements of how Latinos and our nation can ensure an upward trajectory in the years ahead. The first edition was widely influential both as a guide for individuals in their personal quest to reach their potential and as an outline for how our economy can tap the unprecedented Latino reservoir of talent and determination. The second edition provides support for these concepts with current data and examples.

My various responsibilities have taken me across our nation to every one of the fifty states and to more than two hundred U.S. cities. Everywhere I have been I have met the people who make the

American system work. I deeply respect their drive and understand how all those energies come together to move America forward.

I can honestly say that in every one of those places I have met Latinos who are totally capable, equally determined, and admirably hungry to take their places in our nation's economic and social leadership. In their bright eyes, I have seen their ambition to succeed; in their earnest faces, I have seen their desires to help their families and future generations; and in their fierce expressions, I have seen their readiness to work hard, to learn, to put in the necessary hours. I know our national Latino community, and I understand that to unleash its full potential, all our people need is the opportunity, some guideposts, some safety rails, and some trodden paths marked by those who have broken the trail before them. That is precisely what Rodriguez and Tapia have provided.

Theirs is an admirable effort. The future of America will not be determined by people who having climbed the ladder of success and then pulled it up or closed the door behind them. It will not be enhanced by a few stars at the top of the pyramid, enjoying economic comforts and adulation. Rather, a truly prosperous and inclusive American future is in the hands of those who share their knowledge, who hold out a lifeline, and who broaden the upward steps of the societal pyramid at ever-increasing heights. That is what *Auténtico* seeks to do. That is what Rodriguez and Tapia are doing.

Latinos on their upward climb should study the principles set forth in *Auténtico*. American leaders who seek the best for their companies and for American society should integrate those principles into their company strategies and management practices. We would all do well to pay heed.

Rodriguez and Tapia will succeed in this endeavor because their interwoven principles of vision, planning, self-esteem, hard work, lifetime self-improvement, cooperation, and mutual support have always succeeded in the American story.

They have given us an advance look at how Latinos will help write the next chapter of the great American story of progress and inclusion.

Henry Cisneros is the former Mayor of San Antonio and former Secretary of the U.S. Department of Housing and Urban Development. He is chairman of American Triple I, an infrastructure investment firm based in New York.

Ensuring a Vibrant Latino Future

I t was seemingly an era ago that our first edition of *Auténtico* was released in 2017. It was before the coronavirus blew everything to smithereens and before George Floyd's murder ignited a massive racial reckoning.

These tectonic forces that affected all members of society had important particularities in how it affected Latinos in the U.S. Latinos, along with Blacks, ended up being three times more likely to contract the virus, and two times more likely to die of it compared to Whites.[1] The economic implosion due to the pandemic also hit Latinos disproportionately. According to the Bureau of Labor Statistics, Latino unemployment hit 10.3 percent (vs 7 percent for Whites) as of September 2020.[2] Given socioeconomic vulnerabilities, Latinos were among the most likely to be evicted for not being able to pay rent[3] or have to drop out of school due to not having enough bandwidth to keep up with online classes.[4]

All this on top of four years of escalating hateful anti-immigrant rhetoric and acts, including cruel and dehumanizing separation of families and incarcerations in cages. Meanwhile, nearly one million young Latinos eligible for the Deferred Action for Childhood Arrivals (DACA) program, who have known only the U.S. as their country, continued in a legal limbo that impedes their ability to realize the fullness of their potential as well as to fully secure their economic well-being. Also, the deportations, the incarcerations, and the legal status uncertainties, as well as the way the decennial U.S. Census was conducted—with manipulations of data collection scheduling and fear-inducing tactics (like attempts to add a citizenship question in the questionnaire)—led to both fewer Latinos to count, and fewer Latinos who were counted.

On top of all this came the racial injustice reckoning, as protests exploded across the country to denounce the deaths of George Floyd, Breonna Taylor, and Ahmaud Arbery as only the latest victims of police brutality. While the protests have raised awareness of social injustices faced by the African-American community, Latinos have struggled to find ways to bring similar attention to the plight faced by the Hispanic community in a manner that does not come across as taking away from the urgent and vital need to focus on Black equality, dignity, and safety.

During this time and in the wake of it all, in corporate America Latinos have had a mixed and complex experience. For many Latinos, working from home and being on Zoom all the time tore down the curtain they had carefully erected to keep their very culturally different home lives separate from their corporate lives. At the same time, the attention on racial justice and systemic racism triggered by the Black Lives Matter movement began to widen the aperture in some corporate mind-sets. Latinos, they realized, were also being overlooked and needed to be brought into the conversations and efforts, recognizing that the headwinds both groups face converge as well as diverge.

Finally, there was the election of 2020. And even though Hispanics tend to vote Democratic, President Trump polled well in certain Latino communities, including Hispanics in south Florida who liked Trump's tough stance on Cuba's and Venezuela's socialism.

Throughout all of these crises, Latinos continue to persist, endure, and hope for a positive future. Since our first edition there has been one tiny improvement in our representation on boards and executive management. After six years stuck at 4 percent in both spheres, the latest Hispanic Association on Corporate Responsibility (HACR) study (2020) shows an uptick to 5 percent. Hence the update in chapter 1, changing the "Corporate 4% Shame" to the "Corporate 5% Shame."

It was the overwhelming positive response from readers, corporations, and the marketplace to our first edition that prompted us to produce this second edition with an updated context and statistics. However, as we looked at the findings and original thesis of our work, we found they still were as relevant now as they were a few years ago.

The two of us crisscrossed the country—at first on planes and then for more than a year on virtual platforms due to the pandemic—to consult and speak on these issues and put our findings into practice with clients.

The resonance of our findings with what our audiences were experiencing and feeling was deep and profound.

In particular, we received positive reactions to our overview of the four main archetypes in regard to our sense of Latino identity, the ways in which archetypical Latino and archetypical corporate America cultures clash, our cultural ambivalence about ambition, and the comparative study between Latino and Black attitudes toward power.

Our Latino Executive Manifesto has also received much prominent attention among Latino professional networks, employee/resource network groups, corporate C-suites, and the media, such as with *Hispanic Executive* magazine and *CNN en Español*. This call to action, articulating what needs to happen in order to ensure a more vibrant Latino future, has been embraced by both Hispanics and our non-Hispanic allies.

The momentum of the first edition led to publishing the book in Spanish as well as in eBook format. We also published a workbook titled *Be Auténtico*, to help those who wish to explore their Hispanic identity more deeply through various reflective exercises.

Auténtico has also become part of the core curriculum in the two-day Latino Leadership Intensive (LLI) program. The LLI is delivered annually at various universities across the country, including Stanford University in Palo Alto, California, and DePaul University in Chicago. The main focus of the LLI is to develop traditional leadership capabilities such as decision-making, problem-solving, coaching others, and balancing priorities, with an eye to the Latino cultural script's influence on how Hispanic professionals manifest these capabilities.

Based on our surveys and our on-the-ground work, it is clear that *Auténtico* has helped many realize that the more corporate systems deny Latinos the chance to assume leadership roles, the more these organizations will falter at optimizing the contributions Latinos can make to them. *Auténtico* has helped organizations create environments that will help nurture Latino talent success. We are proud to see greater acknowledgment that Latinos must be allowed to bring their true, authentic selves to the workplace.

For the Latino community, we believe *Auténtico* has helped Latinos realize that no community can lift up another; rather, that elevation must come from within. While we greatly value our non-Hispanic allies, especially those that leverage their position of privilege to help give greater voice to our community, we are keenly aware that we are the ones who must lead the way to fight the injustices faced by Latinos.

We've seen a renewed fire—and a more focused ambition—to elevate more Latinos, so that our representation in leadership positions within corporate America mirrors our numbers and our economic contributions.

We hope that this second edition will further help Latinx professionals look at themselves in the context of corporate America. In doing so, each of us must decide, in the context of our Latino heritage, ¿*Quien soy yo*? (Who am I?). *Auténtico* will help readers see that the energy for change must come first from within. When each of us finds out who we are, then we will know what we have to do.

With this second edition of *Auténtico*, we recommit ourselves to doing our part in ensuring a more vibrant Latino future.

Latino? Latina? Hispanic? Latinx?

S o, what is the right term? many ask.

In this book you will see that we use them all. Sometimes as synonyms, other times with an intended nuanced meaning.

Before we explain those nuances, a little bit of linguistic history.

"Hispanic" was first introduced to mainstream American society during the Nixon administration when a term was developed to capture in the U.S. Census people of Spanish-speaking descendants. At the time an overwhelming percentage of Hispanics in the U.S. were of Mexican descent (either born in this country, immigrants, or descendants of those who had been on Mexican land that was then taken by the U.S. in the Mexican-American War). So, in English, the term "Hispanic" was adopted by many in these mostly Mexican Hispanic communities.

As the number of immigrants from other parts of Latin America grew over the decades, immigrants with no historical ties to the land that is now part of the U.S., who were less likely to have been exposed to English, tended to not favor the English word "Hispanic" to describe themselves and instead favored the Spanish word "Latino." But let's be clear: many of Mexican descent also rejected "Hispanic" due to its English roots and preferred the culturally rooted term "Chicano," which had arisen at the regional epicenter of Southern California.

Hispanic and Latino both became popular, and while many of those of Mexican descent tended to favor "Hispanic" and those from other parts "Latino," neither term has been seen as pejorative, or better or worse linguistically. There was not a sense of evolution of terminology to what would have been considered a more affirming word.

Then in the past five years the term "Latinx" has arrived on the scene, eliciting many mixed emotions. This term evolved as a younger generation challenged the fixed gender-binary connotations of Latino/Latina, feeling it left out those who don't consider themselves either male or female. Plus, they challenged the patriarchal connotation that when there is a group of Latinos and a group of Latinas together they are collectively referred by the masculine "Latino." As for the "x" part of Latinx, it fits with the times, with x currently a trendy suffix that shows up in terms like X-Factor, X Games, Gen X, and so on.

According to Pew Hispanic Research, there are clear generational differences in familiarity with and preference for "Latinx." While only 15 percent of boomers and 19 percent of Gen X have heard of the term, at least 42 percent of millennials and Gen Z have (Pew did not poll Gen Z under age eighteen.[1]) In terms of preference for the term, only 3 percent of Gen X and boomers totally accept or prefer the term Latinx, but more than double of Gen Z and Gen Y prefer it. Clearly there's a generational difference that we must honor on both sides.

So, in this book, we use "Hispanic" and "Latino" interchangeably when it's a generic reference to the demographic group (which one we use is in part influenced by the research or person we were interviewing and their preferred term). We deliberately use "Latino" and "Latina" as often as we can when referring to groups that include both women and men rather than defaulting to the masculine. However, we do not do it every time simply for streamlining purposes where we felt using "Latino" would not be exclusionary in the context.

When referring to the boomer executives, we tended to use Hispanic/Latino/Latina. But when referring to younger professionals who were the subjects of our focus groups and our younger professional profiles, we deliberately used "Latinx" when referring to them, given their greater preference for that term.

Those are the choices we made. If you are wondering which term you should use, for those of you who are Latinos/Latinas/Hispanics/Latinx, it's your choice. And for those not from this heritage, when in doubt, just ask. You will get different answers from different people and that's OK. Just honor and respect how they have chosen to self-identify.

The Coming Latino Talent Boom and the Urgency for More Latino Executives

"Pies, ¿para qué los quiero si tengo alas pa' volar?"

Feet, what do I need you for when I have wings to fly?

—Frida Kahlo, Mexican painter

Why this book now? Because there are more than sixty million Latinos, around forty-eight million of whom are U.S. citizens. They are transforming American society—in politics, in the economy, and in the workplace—in underestimated ways.

But there are definitely too few Latino executives and senior leaders, and this must change. To do so, we need to be vigilant in defense and savvy on offense.

Defense is about neutralizing the many conscious and unconscious biases toward Latinos that create obstacles and then relentlessly diminishing them in decision-makers' thought patterns. Also, we must surface how these biases have been systematized in the ways talent sourcing, recruiting, retention, development, and advancement effectively sideline Latino and other traditionally underrepresented talent from rising to the top echelons of leadership.

While that work gets done, we must also move on offense. A key component that contributes to Latino advancement is highlighting successful Latino role models and the keys to their success that can be passed on to the next generation of rising Latino leaders.

Inspired by Price Cobbs's seminal work on the secrets of successful Black leaders, *Cracking the Corporate Code: The Revealing Success Stories of 32 African-American Executives,*[1] we set out to research and write a Latino version of the corporate success narrative.

To do so, we interviewed twenty successful boomer executives, and dozens of Gen X and millennial Latinos and Latinas. As we listened to their stories of *éxito* (success) we looked for themes—convergences and divergences in what they faced in their career paths, how they addressed the challenges, and how they seized the opportunities—and with their narratives we captured the lessons learned that can be used by future Latino leaders.

In addition, we focused on Latino executives who retained their sense of Latino identity throughout their careers and, in fact, used it as an asset in their ascendancy and effectiveness in their work. To us this cultural identity grounding was the basis of their being *auténtico* (authentic), a hallmark that contemporary leadership research reveals as a foundation for being a successful twenty-first-century leader.[2]

The Context of Rising Latino Presence

Before diving into the leadership stories and the lessons they offer, discussing the context of the rising Latino presence in the U.S. is important.

Latinos are changing the popular culture, the marketplace, and the political landscape. Consider this: in the first decade of the twenty-first century, the number of Latinos increased at three times the growth rate of the rest of the population. Latinos are now the largest ethnic minority group, at 18.5 percent of the country's population, and comprise 21 percent of the millennial generation. Latinos accounted for half of the overall U.S. population growth. At this rate Latinos are expected to make up 21 percent of the U.S. population by 2030 and one-fourth by 2050. By 2060, the U.S. Hispanic population is estimated to reach 128.8 million.

Analyze the meaning of this large and growing Latino presence as it relates to professional advancement. Today Latinos represent 17 percent of the U.S. workforce and have a participation rate of roughly 66 percent. This is a higher workforce participation rate than among European Americans, African Americans, or Asians. Further, Latinos are expected to comprise 20 percent of the workforce by 2042 and these are not just blue-collar jobs. Latino high school graduates are enrolling in college at a higher rate than ever before and are poised to be the most highly educated generation of Hispanic Americans in U.S. history.[3] This percentage is not just a student body ratio; it is the future workforce.

Latinos will not only make their presence known in the workplace, but—as *Time* magazine declared in a September 15, 2016, feature story—they are also on pace to "…drive America's economic growth."[4] Some related highlights include:

- In 2020, Latinos, at 18.5 percent of the U.S. population, are estimated to have $1.7 trillion in purchasing power, surpassing the GDP of Mexico and growing at a rate of $100 billion a year as they move to become over one-quarter of the U.S. population by 2060.

- For the decade 2009–2019, Hispanics accounted for 51.6 percent of U.S. net homeownership growth.
- From 2009 through 2019, the number of Latino business owners grew 34 percent, compared to 1 percent for all business owners in the United States.
- Collectively, Latino-owned companies that employ others generated about $470 billion in revenue and employed over 3.2 million people in 2016, accounting for about 4 percent of U.S. business revenues and 5.5 percent of U.S. employment (Figure 1).

The Hispanic market is not just a niche market; it is the market.

On the political front, Latinos played a meaningful role in the last three presidential elections. They helped elect Barack Obama twice and were then a central issue on both sides of the debate in Donald Trump's election. In 2016, 13 percent of the electorate was Hispanic/Latino, up from 11 percent in 2012, 9 percent in 2008, and 7 percent in the 2010 midterms. Between 2008 and 2016, the number of eligible Latino voters grew from 19.5 million to 27.3 million, a 40 percent increase.[5] Eligible Latino voters will number an impressive 30 million in the next election cycles. This is not a side constituency; it is a potential margin of victory.

The massive Latinization of the U.S. has reached every fabric of American culture from food to music to entertainment. On Latino influence of mainstream culture, we have Jorge Ramos on Univision anchoring the most-watched newscast among *all* networks. Pitbull tops the charts time after time with cross-ethnic, cross-cultural collaborations. Salsa has long surpassed the all-American ketchup as the number one condiment in the U.S. Peruvian cuisine is garnering top restaurant status in some American cities. Andean quinoa is as ubiquitous as Quaker oatmeal.

The Gap

Yet as Latinos increase their presence in the marketplace, popular culture, and political arena, they do not find prospects as bright in the workplace. According to the Hispanic Association on Corporate Responsibility (HACR), in their 2019 Corporate Inclusion Index, Latinos held just over 8 percent of board seats among participating companies and a little more than 5 percent of executive officer positions.

On boards this is only a marginal improvement from HACR's 2016 Corporate Inclusion Index when Latinos held only 7 percent of corporate board seats among HACR's participating companies, and pretty much unchanged in the number of Latinos in executive officer positions.[6]

Behind these low representation numbers, a 2013 Harris Interactive poll found that over 75 percent of Latinos feel people with their background are discriminated against by not being hired or promoted for a job and being called names or insulted. According to a 2016 study published by the Center for Talent Innovation, *Latinos at Work: Unleashing the Power of Culture*, most Latinos in the U.S. do not feel that they can bring their whole sense of Latino-ness to the office. The study found that the vast majority of Latinos (76 percent) repress parts of their personas at work.

In spite of these headwinds, as college-educated Latinos become a greater percentage of the available labor force, companies who are unsuccessful at sourcing, attracting, and engaging this talent pool will see their talent pipeline shrivel up. Corporations sit at the edge of a yawning talent divide when it comes to Latinos in the U.S. While the number of Latino executives is still very small in corporate corridors of power, Latino talent is burgeoning—not only in hourly workers but also in the professional ranks. Without a doubt the workforce of the future will have an increasingly Latino identity.

FIGURE 1

Latino Share of the U.S. Population

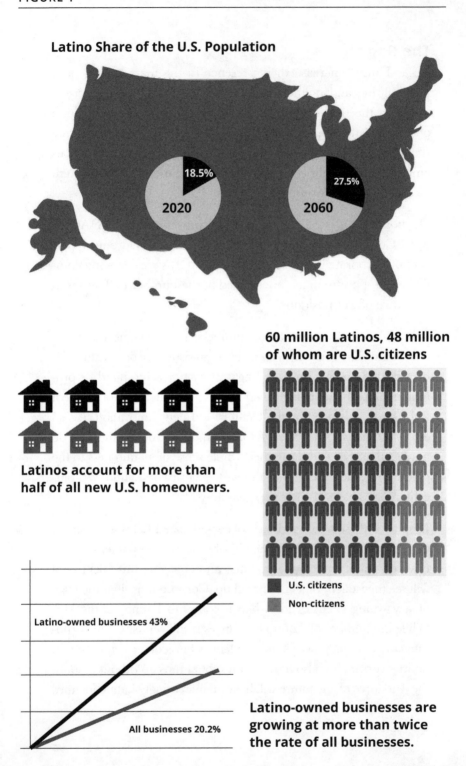

18.5%
2020

27.5%
2060

Latinos account for more than half of all new U.S. homeowners.

60 million Latinos, 48 million of whom are U.S. citizens

U.S. citizens
Non-citizens

Latino-owned businesses 43%

All businesses 20.2%

Latino-owned businesses are growing at more than twice the rate of all businesses.

In 2020 U.S. Latinos had $1.7 trillion in purchasing power, surpassing the GDP of Mexico

This number is increasing by numbers that are close to $100 billion per year

Jorge Ramos of Univision anchors the most-watched newscast among all networks—and has won eight Emmys

In 2016, 13 percent of the electorate was Hispanic/Latino, up from 11 percent in 2012, and 9 percent in 2008

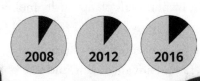

Let's Look at Latino Leaders

Most companies are still asleep at the wheel, failing to recognize that there is an exploding Latino workforce. Even worse, most do not understand what will entice Latinos to come work for them. Companies that wake up to this gap first will be best poised to win the talent war for future generations.

We will start by looking at those leaders who made it in spite of the obstacles. Our book is grounded in primary and secondary research, illustrated by stories of those interviewed, and interpreted through our personal experiences. Ultimately, we seek to offer the keys to success that have served successful Latinos, and to codify what we believe will provide a guide for the next generation of Latino executives.

The research we undertook included the following:

- In-depth interviews with twenty Latino and Latina executives
- A targeted survey completed by a total of twenty Latino executives and senior leaders
- Five focus groups with up-and-coming Latinos and Latinas under age forty in the geographically dispersed locations of New York City, Dallas, Chicago, and Los Angeles
- A targeted survey filled out by hundreds of upwardly mobile Latinos and Latinas
- Secondary research synthesis of over a dozen studies on Latinos in the workplace, Latino advancement, and markers of success
- A journalistic look at major sociocultural, economic, political, and corporate trends that mark the impact the growing Latino presence is having on U.S. society and business

This research approach and the subsequent insights shared in this book were filtered through our own personal and professional journeys. We both have dedicated our careers to the inclusion and advancement of traditionally underrepresented groups. Robert's focus has been on enhancing the effectiveness of employee resource groups in general and in addressing the specifics of Latino talent acquisition, as well as Latino leadership development and advancement. Andrés has focused on enterprise-wide diversity and inclusion strategies and on the leadership development of traditionally unrepresented talent, as well as on improving the capabilities of all executives and senior leaders to lead more inclusively.

We have a collective thirty years of corporate experience in the topic, serving more than two hundred clients. These clients have been in nearly every for-profit sector (retail, finance, manufacturing, managing consultancies), government (regulatory, law enforcement, military, intelligence), healthcare, and not-for-profits (education, social services, advocacy groups). These companies have been domestic as well as global.

We have organized the book in the following way:

Part 1, "Outer Forces: The Challenge of Being Latino in Corporate America," explores the unseen cultural challenges that many Latinos face in their quest to give their best at work and, in doing so, find the pathway to advancement in leadership roles. What are these challenges, why do they exist, and what is the often unintended, yet very real, detrimental impact on the contributions Latinos can make in the workplace?

All this in turn forces identity questions for Latino talent. Should they bury their own unique Latino identity and instead assimilate into the corporate culture, or should they instead double down without apology on what it means for them to be Latino and try not to deny their identity? These are among the most urgent and vexing questions many Latino professionals face today.

With the context set for what it's like to be Latino in corporate America, in Part 2, "Inner Forces: Successful Strategies of Latino Executives," we turn to what we learned from the executives we interviewed, asking how they personally addressed their dilemmas. In listening to them as a cohort, we extracted themes of convergence and divergence. With convergence, we looked at which issues emerged consistently for these successful executives. For divergences, we looked at their journeys and the choices made in their career paths that were not linked to social and cultural patterns but influenced more by each person's personality and uniqueness.

Among the themes we found were the role of education, and how Latino culture can be both an inner asset as well as something that produces dilemmas and challenges in ascending the corporate ladder. We also mapped out what these leaders shared as the keys to becoming a transformative leader.

The lessons learned and bits of advice offered by the boomer executives set the stage for the chapter "The Next Generation of Latino Leaders: Latinx Learns, Challenges, and Rises," where we compare and contrast their experiences and effective strategies with the two Latino generations that followed them: the Gen Xers and millennials. We lay out some fundamental sociohistorical and cultural generational differences and how these affect advancement—or lack of—within their organizations. We identify their needs and techniques for resolving those needs. In addition, we point out how they would benefit from the experience and wisdom of those Latinos who did make it to the top.

Finally, in our conclusion we take a step back from what individuals have done to break through barriers and seize opportunities to look at what government, corporations, not-for-profits, and educational entities can do to address still existing institutional resistance to Latinos and their heritage.

The Feeling of Being Latino

Having outlined the intellectual basis and approach to the book, we have one final word on the soul of this book.

We recognize that there is vast diversity within and across the Latino experience. Latinos, wrote Carlos Fuentes, are *una raza cósmica* (a cosmic race)—a fusion and amalgam of ethnicities, races, social classes, and religions. But through it all there is something intangible, some *esencia* (essence), that captures what it means to be Latin whether we are first, second, third, or fourth generation, boomer, Gen X, or millennial, Spanish dominant or English dominant, or somewhere in between.

This variety is what both of us, Robert and Andrés, also bring to this book. Robert, the son of Mexican immigrants, grew up in Minneapolis without much of a sense of his Latino heritage.

Andrés spent his childhood in Lima, Perú. His Peruvian dad met his American mom during his medical residency at the Cleveland Clinic. They fell in love and married, and when Andrés was a year old, the family moved to Lima, where he grew up and lived until the time finally came for him to attend college in the U.S.

There are the basics of language, food, dress, surnames, and music that Latinos share. However, leaving home is often when the feeling of being Latino is challenged and each must confront this experience in their unique way, navigating a majority European-American culture.

So what is that feeling of being Latino? Let's explore this by taking a short journey into the mysteries of one form of Latin artistic expression: flamenco.

Andrés's twenty-something daughter, Marisela, is a professional flamenco dancer with much formal and informal training including many performances. Recently he joined her in Seville, Spain, the mecca of flamenco, where she was obtaining some master training in this ancient dance form. Like Latino culture itself, flamenco is an amalgam of influences beginning in India and coursing through the Middle East and the Baltics before landing in Moorish Spain.

To his surprise and delight (as well as trepidation), Marisela had enrolled him in a flamenco class during his visit. Knowing that this twelve-beat art form was exceptionally complex in technique, Andrés was skeptical as well as apprehensive about how much he could learn—not to mention how much he could do so without a high level of embarrassment—in the three scheduled sessions.

Marisela explained that this was the perfect class because the accomplished dancer who was the instructor was focused not on the technique of flamenco but on the *feeling* of flamenco. In fact, the instruction takes place with tennis shoes, so students will not be distracted by the drama and performance activation that the flamenco shoes' staccato elicits.

The lessons begin with the music. The instructor, Luis Peña, invites participants to listen, not just with their ears but with their whole body. Then they can allow that physical resonance caused by the guitar string, the *canto* (flamenco singing), and *palmas* (rhythmic hand clapping) to elicit a feeling. Only at that time should they release their bodies to move in response to *la música*. Their feet will find the beat, their hands and arms will channel the surge that emanates from within, and their heads will swivel in the direction of an invisible presence.

When they have found the feeling—felt it, channeled it—then, and only then, are they in the right place to learn the complex techniques of the seemingly infinite twelve-beat variations of flamenco.

And so it was with Andrés. His uncertain steps and the sense of being in over his head gave way to allowing his feeling for the music to surge through his legs, feet, arms, and hands. Suddenly the surge made his body move in a flamenco way. His technique may have been far from perfect, but there he was in full, true flamenco expression.

Andrés's journey in learning the feeling of flamenco is not unlike the journey to cultural identity that many Latinos face. While there is a concrete aspect to the Latino reality (how to dance salsa, how to prepare *arroz con pollo*, or how to speak Spanish correctly), these are secondary to the feeling of being Latino.

While Andrés grew up with a Latino feeling as a young person in Lima, things were different for Robert. As one of the very few Latinos in Scandinavian Minneapolis, he did not have a strong feeling of Latino-ness. With *mamá's* spices spreading their aroma in the kitchen at home, he experienced some feeling of being a Latino, but he had not internalized it. Robert did not learn Spanish (researchers have proven there is an inextricable link between language and cultural meaning). Nor did he participate in Latin dancing. And what passed for "Mexican" food in Minneapolis did not even come close to the real thing.

Thus, Robert grew up without that Latino feeling. Yet in the middle of his career, he began to long for it, especially after he had begun his research of Latino talent. This work awoke in him a need and a desire to discover that Latino feeling. Just as in Andrés's flamenco class experience, Robert realized that while learning the details of a language or a cuisine was important, being Latino was about a feeling. He began to connect with the artistic vibrations emanating from Latino authors whose works he had not read, and from the music he had heard only with his ears but not his body. He paid more attention to the stories of Latino identity that he heard repeatedly in the course of his work. He also connected more with Latin culture by studying Latin American history and visiting Latin countries including the Dominican Republic, Panama, Ecuador, and Argentina. As he did this, he began to allow the feeling of Latino-ness to course through his body to the point when he knew what being Latino meant. *Lo siento, lo hago* (I feel it, I do it).

That is the spirit of this book. When we talked with these executives and the up-and-coming Latino leaders and saw the patterns in their stories, we not only listened to their words but also sought to capture their feeling of what being Latino means and how they desire to more fully express that Latino-ness.

Welcome to the journey of Latino *éxito*—while remaining *auténtico*.

" Welcome. We love your differences—now be just like us. "

PART **1**

OUTER FORCES:
THE CHALLENGE
OF BEING LATINO IN
CORPORATE AMERICA

Latino executives and aspiring leaders must confront forces both outside of themselves (discrimination, unconscious biases, pressures to conform) and within (sorting out their career aspirations, defining their Latino cultural identity) as they press on to ascend as leaders.

In addition, like other underrepresented groups in corporate America, Latinos face seemingly irreconcilable corporate pressures: on one hand, to assimilate in how they look, talk, and behave; and on the other, in how they handle personal pressures to be different as Latino leaders.

How do they overcome these pressures without burying their own diverse identity for the sake of fitting in?

For many Latinos who come from cultural backgrounds and environments quite different from that of most individuals in corporate America, this dilemma is particularly acute.

Part 1 traces these invisible—yet very real—forces and the different types of trajectories the leaders chose and why, and how corporate America responded. Let's look at how these encounters have led to both conflict and resolution.

CHAPTER 1

The Myths of Meritocracy and Color-Blind Corporate Cultures

Cuando estás convencido que una causa es justa, continua luchando.

When you are convinced a cause is just, keep fighting.

—Rigoberta Menchú, Guatemalan human rights activist
1992 Nobel Peace Prize

Meritocracy—that uplifting concept defined as a workplace ethic that rewards those who show talent and competence as demonstrated by performance—is one of corporate America's most cherished ideologies. According to this value, getting ahead in the workplace is based solely on individual merit.

Latinos and other traditionally underrepresented groups buy into the idea of meritocracy, often pursuing corporate careers precisely due to its promise. The trouble is, when companies consider Latinos and other minority groups, they fall seriously short of living up to this ideal.

Why does this happen? To explore the causes of any system failure, we first must understand how the system is supposed to work.

Meritocracy Design

Merit is generally viewed as a combination of innate abilities, hard work, and intelligence.

The meritocracy ideology is very much aligned with the "American Dream": the U.S. as the land of limitless opportunity where individuals can go as far as their abilities and desires will take them. When placed in a work context, supporters speak glowingly of a singularly meritocratic environment where everyone has equal opportunity and where the workplace is a level playing field. The tenets of meritocracy put work environments on a path that is supposed to be color-blind and gender neutral.

In a meritocracy, a fair and equitable work environment creates a competitive system. Those who outperform their peers get promoted. In a meritocracy, hard work pays off, and each person, judged solely on results, rises to realize their fullest potential. Proponents of a meritocracy say the issues of race, ethnicity, and gender do not matter because merit is all about performance.

Ask most Latino leaders and executives, and they'll tell you they too believe in the meritocracy ideology. In fact, that is what Latinos want. They do not want to be promoted because of their Hispanic ethnicity; rather, they want to get ahead based solely on their capabilities.

Meritocracy Illusion

However, a review of the top of the organization charts and the profile of most corporate boards tells us something is not quite right. If the level playing field is indeed as equitable as meritocracy proclaims, then corporate leadership should mirror the racial, ethnic, and gender makeup of the available labor force. A true meritocracy should espouse proportional representation of all kinds of talent, because the law of averages would be at work. When a meritocracy is real, there should be no shortage of women and people of color in top leadership positions.

Ask any corporate executive—or most members of our society for that matter—if they believe that women and people of color are inherently inferior to European-American men, and the answer is a resounding "no." Indeed, to admit to believing otherwise would be to admit they are racist and sexist.

However, if we as a society don't believe women and racial and ethnic minorities are inferior, and if we believe that a meritocracy is fair and based solely on performance, how then do we explain the paucity of women and people of color in top corporate roles? What could be holding our organizations back from delivering on the promise and the value of the intended outcomes of a meritocracy?

This gap between how society believes people are promoted in our organizations and how organizations actually promote people unveils what we, and various other writers, refer to as the myth of the meritocracy.[1] While considerations of merit do affect some who advance and receive promotions, other forces vastly diminish the perception of merit.

For Latinos in the workplace, the reality is that they don't tend to come from the same backgrounds as the majority culture. In fact, Latinos face different types of headwinds that create a drag on their ability to progress. This and other non-merit factors suppress, neutralize, or even negate the effects of merit, creating barriers to individual Hispanic mobility in corporate America. We must recognize those forces that keep Latinos in roles and positions that they currently occupy regardless of the extent of individual merit.

The 5 Percent Shame

The myth of meritocracy holds that those who "make it" do so because of their excellent ability; in a true meritocracy, what you do, and not who you are, is what matters.

As the HACR 2019 Corporate Inclusion Index (described in the introduction) documented, Latino representation in top roles in corporate America proves that meritocracy is not fulfilling its true promise. Only a little over 5 percent of executive officer positions in Fortune 500 firms are held by Hispanics. Worse news is that Hispanic females hold just 1 percent of those positions. Further, HACR research shows little movement at all in the representation of Hispanics over the past several years.

The myth of meritocracy continues for Hispanics when you review their representation on corporate boards of directors. While HACR's index of participating companies came up with an 8 percent representation, the Alliance for Board Diversity reports that Hispanics/Latinos held only 3.5 percent of Fortune 500 board seats in 2016. In either case, whether 3.5 or 7 percent, this is a woeful gap from the 17 percent representation of Latinos in the U.S. population. This is not to suggest that the percentage of board positions needs to be 17 percent at this time, since we do need to account for an eligible pool with certain educational and leadership credentials. However, while we must still address the legacy of educational disparities, this yawning 10 to 13.5 percent gap cannot be explained away simply with the "there's not an available labor pool" argument.

If a meritocracy is supposed to result in a normal distribution of leadership opportunity based on merit, then companies must address what we refer to as "the 5 percent shame." Something besides merit is preventing Latino and Hispanic advancement to these executive officer positions in Fortune 500 firms. The gap points to the existence of favoritism, discrimination, and bias in most corporate cultures. Supporters of a meritocracy don't realize that the current system reinforces ideals that shore up existing power structures and privileges.

We must also think through the pressures faced by those 4 percent of Hispanic and Latino executives who have demonstrated merit and moved to the very top of the corporate ladder. Their relative scarcity at the top of a meritocracy system places them under a microscope for other Latinos in the workplace who are desperate for role models who look like them. Many of these Latino executives may prefer to simply not be identified by their ethnic affiliation so they can avoid being associated with what they perceive as negative stereotypes that members of the majority may have of Latinos. At the same time, the organization is eager to highlight their presence in leadership ranks as what turns out to be false evidence that the meritocracy system does indeed work for Latinos.

Latino executives who do not appear to connect strongly with their ethnicity or who are not seen actively advocating for Hispanic issues may be inadvertently sending a message to younger Latinos that the road to success within a meritocracy requires assimilation and the denial of their Hispanic heritage.

Data suggests that this phenomenon is already happening. In the 2016 study conducted by the Center for Talent Innovation (highlighted in the introduction), we saw that more than three out of four Latinos expend energy repressing parts of their persona in the workplace, downplaying their ethnicity. Having to expend energy related to their identity means that energy is not available for use in improving their workplace performance, thus lowering their chances of success. Some could conclude that Latino executives who chose not to connect visibly with their Hispanic identity in the workplace are unintentionally complicit in the myth of meritocracy.

Conscious and Unconscious Bias

These realities of Latinos experiencing discrimination and bias in the workplace undermine the promise of meritocracy. Several of the Latino leaders interviewed for this book described experiencing conscious bias in the workplace. As an example, one of our Hispanic executive interviewees described an outing with an executive from a previous employer:

> We went to this Hispanic event together, and at the event we were selling our product. As he was walking around he said, "What are these people wearing? Do they even have cars to drive?" So, I said to him, "You know I think it's best you leave because you're probably going to do more damage to our company's brand than good at this point, and what you said is extremely offensive." So he left the event. Fast-forward a week after and he announced a reorganization, and the result of the whole reorganization was the elimination of just one job—and that job was mine.

Darren Rebelez, current president and CEO of Casey's General Stores, recalls working many years ago at a different company whose leader was in his mid-seventies. While at an informal work gathering, someone innocently asked Darren about his ethnicity, to which Darren responded that he was Mexican. He described this leader's response on hearing his answer:

> He said, "No, you're not Mexican." I said, "Well, sure I am." Again, he said, "No, you are not a Mexican." I didn't realize it until that moment, but he was a bigot. The notion that a Mexican could have risen to such a high level within the company, it just blew his mind.

Luis Ubiñas, former senior partner at McKinsey & Company, past president of the Ford Foundation, and current corporate board member and advisor, adds this experience:

> I say this with no bitterness, but what you need to remember is that we don't come from a place where race doesn't matter. I remember being at a meeting, as one of McKinsey's leading experts on newspapers, where the head of a small regional newspaper turned to the senior partner who's introducing me to them and said to my face, "Is this the best you can do?" All he knew about me was that I was Hispanic.

While examples of conscious bias such as these may not be rampant, their negative impact on Latino upward mobility in the workplace can be formidable. Just a handful of stories become part of the corporate lore, which then gets repeated a hundredfold.

Equally impactful is the unconscious bias Latinos face at work. That bias permeates the workplace at all levels because we all have prejudices. Numerous studies confirm that people harbor unconscious bias even when they explicitly believe that prejudice and discrimination are wrong.

Unconscious bias is subtler but often no less corrosive to Latinos attempting to reach the fullness of their own potential. Even well-intentioned people who wouldn't say they are biased sometimes display unconscious bias against Latinos, assuming certain inaccurate stereotypes, and potentially hurting Latinos' career advancement. Victor Arias, managing director at Diversified Search, recalled a meeting he had with a previous employer earlier in his career. The meeting, scheduled in a conference room, was with the CEO of the company at that time:

> I walked into the meeting at the appropriate time and on the table there is a meal place setting. Then the CEO came in and he said, "Well, I think it's really important that we teach you how to have lunch." I was very insulted. I just said, "You are making the assumption that I don't know this already." "No, no, no," he said. I asked, "Do you do this for everybody?" His response? "No."

And there was the time he walked into the locker room of the upscale health club he belonged to and another member attempted to hand him some wet towels and asked him to bring some dry ones. Victor set him straight.

Acts of unconscious bias lead people to wrongly assume that Latinos are not leaders. One Latina executive interviewed for this book describes some of the meetings she attends where such bias is still on display:

> I've had vendors come and present to me and to my team, and these vendors assume that I'm not the one making the final decision. When they present, they looked at everyone else but me. When I ask questions, they would look at others and answer the question. That's usually when I just get up, walk away, and not finish the meeting.

These biases create additional headwinds that some Latinos are not able to overcome because it saps their motivation. Misunderstandings may arise when cultural differences in how Latinos respond to feedback, prefer to complete their tasks, and express emotions may make their non-Latino managers uncomfortable because those managers come from different sociopsychological backgrounds. (We will look at these specifics in chapter 4.)

The Shadow of Anti-Immigration Walls

The current sociocultural environment in the U.S., which has deliberately stirred up anti-immigrant sentiments and policies, makes it even more difficult to overcome the myth of meritocracy. Most Latinos will not soon forget the statements Donald Trump made during his announcement speech for his candidacy for U.S. president in June 2015:

> When Mexico sends its people, they're not sending their best. . . . They're sending people that have lots of problems, and they're bringing those problems with us. They're bringing drugs. They're bringing crime. They're rapists. And some, I assume, are good people.

This set the tone for YouTube video clips capturing incidents across the country of people telling Latinos to "Go back to where you came from," or demanding "Why don't you learn to speak English?" Newspapers routinely publish stories of increased violence about Latinos or Latino schools being vandalized with graffiti that reads, "Build the wall higher."

These sentiments also convey perceived negative economic costs associated with job competition and an undue burden on education and social services. While some anti-immigration advocates won't admit it, there is a concern that Latino immigrants will cause a change to traditional American identities and values.

Anti-immigrant legislative bills are being driven by isolated incidents of crimes committed by undocumented immigrants (which, by the way, are at half the rate of those committed by citizens)[2] as justification to eliminate sanctuary cities and to enforce harsh immigration policies. The increase in immigration raids is creating fear and stress within the broader Latino community. A recent study by Dr. Edward D. Vargas, published in a 2017 issue of the *Journal of Health Politics, Policy and Law*,[3] found that Latinos who believe that where they live is unfavorable toward immigrants are 70 percent more likely to report poor health, regardless of their own legal or immigration status. Additionally, the study found that Latinos who know about a family member or friend being deported are one and a half times more likely to report needing to seek help for emotional or mental health problems such as feeling anxious, sad, or nervous.

Arrests happen while people are at home, when they drop off their children at school, or when they receive a speeding ticket. Planeloads of deported Latinos regularly land in Mexico City; these are people who came to the U.S. when they were very young; they don't know Spanish, and culturally they see themselves as Americans.

This anti-immigrant sentiment is definitely being noticed by Hispanic executives. Grace Lieblein, former president of General Motors Mexico and current director on the boards of Southwest Airlines and Honeywell, told us:

> I think it's scary. It [anti-immigrant sentiment] worries me, it really does. It worries me from a lot of different perspectives. It makes me feel very unsettled… and I think it's very sad.

Many Hispanic executives fear that such negative sentiment may make it more difficult for Latinos to advocate for Hispanic inclusion and equality in an increasingly polarized country. Such sentiments may make even more Latinos want to downplay or hide their Hispanic heritage, because a growing number of people in the U.S. are equating being Hispanic with being somehow "less than."

Latino Response

Even though anti-immigrant rhetoric appears to undermine Hispanic achievement and progress, conscious and unconscious biases still create obstacles to overcome, our corporate cultures are clearly not color-blind, and meritocracy has its limits, Hispanics are not giving up hope.

Luis Ubiñas reminds Latinos not to let bias or discrimination beat them:

> Any Hispanic who tells you they haven't been exposed to moments of inequity is not telling the truth. The question isn't "Are you going to face moments of discrimination?" but rather "What are you going to do when you do?" Are you going to let them be barriers, or are you going to let them be a motivation? Of course, I've faced discrimination; of course, every Hispanic has faced discrimination. Is that a problem? Of course! Is it something that should be a barrier to Hispanic success? Of course not! Latinos need to ask themselves if they will use discrimination as an excuse to lamely lie down and fail, or are they going to use it as motivation? Remember, at the end of the day this country has been built by people who were first excluded and then led.

In spite of all this, today's Hispanic executives still believe in the power of meritocracy and of the American Dream. Their grandparents, parents, and even some of these executives themselves gave up too much in their immigrant journey in a quest for success to simply stand by and let those dreams be denied—or taken away.

The setbacks have made them more determined than ever to hold corporate America accountable to the idea that Latinos can reach positions of leadership.

CHAPTER 2

Identity Crisis: Assimilate, Opt Out, or Double Down?

Uno no puede pelear consigo mismo, porque esta batalla tendría un solo perdedor.

One can't fight with oneself, since this battle has only one loser.

—Mario Vargas Llosa, Peruvian author 2010 Nobel Prize in Literature

Being Latino is as much about the choices as it is about the heritage. This means that Latino identity relies heavily on how individuals choose to deal with their cultural surroundings. They can accept and internalize them, deny them, or change them.

Choosing is more complex, because Latinos face a myriad of pressures in their journey to define themselves in a society that often disparages their identity and seeks to impose definitions on them rather than allow self-identification. This identity struggle often gets carried into the corporate world experience of many Latino professionals.

This struggle was experienced by many Latino executives in our research study, who at some point had to come to grips with their own sense of Latino identity and ways to express it in the workplace or even try to hide it during certain phases of their careers. The executives who did not lose their Latino identity along the way navigated these difficult organizational waters. Throughout this book we will share the lessons they learned.

This key "to be or not to be" choice point for the Latino executives was at the heart of the professional journey of many of the leaders we interviewed. The confluence of cultural and family pride currents flowing from one side, and of stinging discrimination currents flowing from the other, presented continuous dilemmas on how to best manage their own expression of cultural identity in the workplace.

Exploring how they dealt with these crosscurrents is further complicated because there is little uniformity in the formative years of these leaders. For some, their early years were fully immersed in Latino culture; for others, they were the minority, sometimes the only one, in a mostly European-American culture. Further, a handful of others grew up in racially mixed environments with Blacks, Asians, and other minorities.

Thus there are multiple variations in how the executives dealt with their cultural identity when confronted with stark choices about whether to assimilate, opt out, or double down as they pursued their ambitions to be leaders in their organizations.

In their seminal 2001 essay "Racial Identity Development and Latinos in the United States,"[1] Bernardo Ferdman and Plácida Gallegos describe Latino identity as the lens through which Latinos "see" themselves. The messages that Latinos receive about their group can be positive, negative, or neutral, depending on the identity lens they choose to use.

Based on our research and personal observation, we have categorized the different lenses used and paths Latinos leaders have taken as follows:

UNAPOLOGETIC LATINOS
Have fully embraced their Latino identity and chosen not hide it, even in the most non-Latino of environments.

EQUIVOCAL LATINOS
Have some boundaries about their Latino identity because of European-American values they were heavily exposed to in their formative years and in the course of their educational and career pursuits.

RETRO LATINOS
May have grown up as an Equivocal Latino but, for a variety of reasons in adulthood, have gone back to their Latino roots to discover or rediscover those elements of a distant or submerged heritage and culture.

INVISIBLE LATINOS
Have fully denied and disowned any connection to Latino culture deliberately, whether they grew up in a Latino environment or not.

In our sample of leaders, we found all of the first three types, but it's no surprise that we found no Invisible Latinos. By the very nature of this book's subject, those agreeing to be interviewed came to the conversation with a sense of ownership and pride in their Latino heritage.

As we will see, their stories varied in terms of their upbringing, their journeys of Latino identity, and their resulting positions as leaders. Yet almost all, at some point in their educational and work journeys, had been confronted with a need to *choose* how much their Latino heritage would be part of their leadership identity.

In contrast to Black executives, who by the very nature of the color of their skin don't have a choice, many non-Afro-Latino leaders do have a choice of how much their Latino heritage will be part of their leadership identity.

Because Latinos are not one racial group, but rather an ethnic group that combines races including White, Indigenous, Asian, and Black, some can *pass* as a member of the majority culture if they so choose. Therefore most of the Latino executive stories we collected brim with self-aware narratives of multiple choices made along the way.

The Unapologetic Latino

The stories of two of our leaders—Lisa Garcia Quiroz, former senior vice president of cultural investments at Time Warner, and Victor Arias, managing director for Diversified Search— illustrate the leader who chooses to double down on their ethnic identity when faced with conscious or unconscious peer pressure to assimilate.

To understand their stance, one must first know the story of their formative years. Here is Lisa's narrative of growing up in a fully Latino household in the midst of a White working-class neighborhood, and the way this shaped her own sense of Latina identity. Both the arc as well as the details of her story contain the anchors for her daily decisions as a leader to be unapologetically Latina in how she presents herself:

> I grew up on Staten Island, New York. I'm the oldest of three. My mother is Puerto Rican; my father is the son of Mexican immigrants.

I grew up in a very Latino household. It was like the dichotomy to the external world I lived in. I spoke Spanish before I spoke English. My mother had only been here from Puerto Rico for a couple of years, and she barely spoke English by the time I was born, so I grew up with a strong sense of both the Mexican and Puerto Rican cultures. Growing up, a lot of people would ask me if I felt more Puerto Rican or more Mexican. I felt both equally.

We'd spend weeks at a time in Puerto Rico in a rural part of the island. And my Mexican grandmother ensured that we all grew up with a strong sense of our Mexican roots, which meant that if Tony Aguilar was coming into Madison Square Garden, off we'd go. She was a great cook, so we grew up with the food, the music, and the culture. Then we had these epic trips where she'd take us to Mexico for a few months at a time to make sure we knew where we'd come from.

These connections to our roots were pivotal for my identity because growing up in such a White neighborhood with both overt and unconscious racism, they were what allowed me to survive and even thrive in that environment. It gave me such a strong sense of self and pride about who I was and where I came from that nothing could shake that. This was so important, especially when I think of how easy it would've been for my parents to have said, "No, no, no, no, no—we're going to raise you only as an American."

When you look at my school pictures, I was like the one brown spot in my kindergarten class, my first grade class, my second, and third. Because I was also a really good student, including being the valedictorian of my elementary school class, I got into a great high school, an all-girls Catholic school on Staten Island, where I was a top student. I then went on to Harvard and Harvard Business School. Even today, as the only Latina in the C-suite at Time Warner, the situation is consistent with how it's always been all my life: one brown spot.

Victor Arias also grew up in a Latino household, but, in contrast to Lisa, he was mostly part of a majority Latino culture in El Paso, Texas. He had some adjusting to do when he entered business school and the mostly Anglo and privileged world of Stanford University. He did so while still maintaining his deep Latino roots, sometimes with surprising outcomes.

I grew up in El Paso, Texas, known as the "Ellis Island of the South" because that place has so many families that have gone through there as a transition ground before they took off to different parts of the U.S. Although El Paso is in the U.S., the community is very Mexican. My first language at home was Spanish. Every Sunday we went to Mass, listened to Mexican music, and either hung out with the *abuelos* (grandparents) or visited with friends and shopped in Ciudad Juarez.

So it was very much a bifurcated existence because on the one hand, it was all Spanish, but when you started going to school, you had to know English. My growing up was in a very safe environment with a very big family. My mom came from a family of fourteen, so I had lots of *primos* (cousins) and incredible grandparents. My dad was only one of two, so he gravitated to my mother's side of the family because it was just so special to have so many *hijos* and *hijas* (sons and daughters) and relatives.

My grandmother from my dad's side was a role model of how you can survive. She was a single mom who had come from Chihuahua, Mexico. My dad and my *tía* (aunt) were both born in El Paso, where they lived in a two-room apartment with an outhouse in the back. When we spent the night with my grandmother, we were all cramped up, and I remember having to go to the bathroom at night in the dark to the outhouse with the *cucuy* (boogeyman). As I reminisce about those times of hardship and her work as a domestic, I just remember what those experiences meant for her and her dignity. I know that background impacted my dad, who was a latchkey kid since his mother had to work all day. It set the tone for my dad's motivations to achieve things for us that he didn't have growing up. It gave him drive, energy, and persistence, yet he was always sincere and humble.

My friends were predominantly Latinos, mostly Hispanic in a community like El Paso, but my first experience with mixed cultures was when I went to a Catholic grade school that was supposed to be a good school where there was a good mix of Anglos and Mexicanos. I'd hang out with Anglo friends and that's how I learned a lot of things about them.

Growing up in El Paso, a lot of "Spanglish" was spoken. It was different from the very proper Spanish that my compadres from Ciudad Juarez on the Mexico side would speak. In some ways they would look down on us because we didn't speak Spanish. So I started to feel that kind of difference. Also, most of the guys from Ciudad Juarez came from privileged families, and I felt a little discomfort with that.

Then it came time for Victor to leave familiar El Paso and go to Stanford to get his MBA. This was his first time truly feeling different.

My first day at Stanford I headed to a wine and cheese reception feeling intimidated and thinking, *What the hell am I doing here?* So I wore my best dark blue velour sweatsuit and my best baseball cap. I found this guy who said, "I want you to meet these other friends of mine." So I said, "OK," and he took me over to the middle of the courtyard with all these guys who were the height of preppiness. The last guy, about six-foot-four, sandy-haired, had brown corduroy pants, Topsiders (which I just called boat shoes), two Izod shirts with collars turned up, and a sweater draped over his shoulders. I said to him, "Kurt, how are you? Nice to meet you. Do you have any idea the collars are up on your shirt?" I went behind him and turned his collars down. He got really red. The others thought I was messin' with him.

They said, "Wow, this guy is really bold and kind of crazy to do that." From that day, I got accepted by the rest, and they became my best friends, though Kurt didn't talk to me for two years.

Throughout their exceptionally successful educational trajectories and their stellar careers, neither Lisa nor Victor lost their sense of being Latino; in fact, it is a salient characteristic of their identities in the workplace. Here's Lisa again:

> I had a very strong commitment to ensuring that there were more Latinos and Latinas when I left than when I came in. I will tell you that's been a theme in my life, certainly in my corporate life: not just bringing in more Latinos, but bringing in more people of color as well as more women to any position I have available. My staff is 100-percent diverse. I always want to leave a place better than when I got there.

There are other Unapologetic Latino executives in our sample group whose formative experience stories were quite different—growing up outside the U.S. and immigrating as young adults, or having been an expat in different countries due to their parents' work, or coming from more middle-class backgrounds—but they too are grounded in their ethnic cultural identity. They expressed no ambivalence about it. For example, Paul Raines, former CEO of GameStop, who was born and raised in Costa Rica, shares:

> First of all, Spanish is a beautiful language. In many ways, much, much richer than English. You know, I'm blessed because my mother was one of these people who insisted I speak Spanish as a kid. I see kids today and they sort of go, "Aah, not sure I wanna be speaking Spanish." And I say, "Man, you are missing the greatest opportunity. Nobody says you have to exclude English so you can speak Spanish. What you should be thinking is *I want to be multilingual.*"

Yet to be successful in corporate America, these people with diverse backgrounds also had to find ways to adapt to the very different and contrasting patterns of being, acting, and speaking that are part of any corporate culture. In fact, the overuse of the unapologetic approach can lead to being misunderstood, not fully accepted, or less effective as leaders.

"I feel that when we're in the corporate world we have to tone down our more expressive selves, for it doesn't allow us to be as authentic in what we're trying to project to the people we're working with," a young Latina professional told us at the focus group we conducted at the University of Southern California (USC) in Los Angeles.

A key attribute of Unapologetic Latinos is that they can appreciate the beauty of being Latino and at the same time recognize certain features—those attributed to Latinos that others may perceive as negative—and adjust accordingly without being any less Latino.

Juan Galarraga, a senior vice president at Five Below who grew up in Venezuela and came to the U.S. as an adult, concurs:

> We are loud, we like to challenge, we tell it like it is, and in multiple households, at dinner or wherever, that's how we talk. We're not really fighting, but Anglos often think we are.

So has he adapted?

> Yes, I have. As I've grown in different professional roles, I've realized that our forwardness is one of those areas where it can really hurt us. I do take a lot of pride in what I have to offer, but my *how* in how I present myself has changed over time.

> Maybe instead of making a strong statement such
> as, "I think this is stupid," I may ask an open-ended
> question to lead folks in the room to say, "This may
> not be right."

Another cultural preference that is especially true for Latinos who grew up outside the U.S. is a different sense of what being on time means. Juan says:

> We tend to be late to many events. It's normal; it's
> who we are and how we are. If we say come at 7, we
> would never come at 7; we'd come at 7:30 or 8. But
> at work you have to be cautious of that habit, so I
> have adjusted, and you'll never see me being late to a
> meeting in the U.S.

In a New York City focus group we conducted with Latino and Latina millennial leaders, a young media professional spoke of watching his parents begin to deny their Cuban heritage when they moved to Florida from New York. This was at the time he was beginning to embrace his Latino heritage unapologetically, in direct contrast to his parents:

> My parents are snowbirds now. They loathe Miami.
> My dad refuses to speak Spanish when he's there. He
> hates the fact that he gets better service when he hits
> 2 for Spanish than when he hits 1 for English. He is
> hardcore. "Why are you assuming when I walk into
> CVS that you should be speaking to me in Spanish?"
> my dad wonders.

The Unapologetic Latinos can maintain their cultural selves while still being sensitive and compassionate toward others.

However, these Unapologetic Latinos are always crystal clear about who they are, as summarized by Sandra Rivera, the chief people officer at Intel:

> I do feel like one of my big responsibilities is to make sure, in all of my leadership talks and all the mentoring and sponsorship that I do of Intel employees, that I bring up my Colombian identity as part of who I am. I talk about it in a very public way, so that Latinos who have similar backgrounds can feel proud as well.

The Equivocal Latino

The profile for those we refer to as Equivocal Latinos often emerges from an upbringing where European-American culture was quite predominant in the person's life without deeply infused Latino cultural values being instilled by the family. This often sets the initial parameters of a person's identity. According to Ferdman and Gallegos, for Equivocal Latinos, parents and extended family members tend to instruct the children about the boundaries of their Latino identity. What they learn at home about themselves as Latinos (for example, "We are better than others," or "We are less than others," or "We are no different than others") lays the foundation of their Latino identity.

The *familia* (parents, aunts, grandparents) may have been deeply rooted themselves in the Latino culture, but unlike in Lisa's or Victor's case, the cultural messaging and acculturation was missing or done with a lighter touch. This often takes place because of the parents' desire for their children to be assimilated—and therefore accepted—by mainstream American society. In some of these households, the parents actually chose not to speak Spanish to their children and encouraged them to socialize as much as possible outside the Latin culture because they saw it as an opportunity to increase their children's chances of breaking out of the *barrios* they themselves felt trapped in.

This distancing from Latino culture was further exacerbated when their families chose to move to predominantly non-Latino neighborhoods where the process of acculturation would happen more rapidly and deeply.

Former IHOP President Darren Rebelez grew up in San Diego as a third-generation Latino. His mom was Irish. He comments:

> For me there was more of a heritage in the food than the language. That's one thing I'd harass my dad about all the time; he did not speak Spanish to us. I had to struggle learning it on my own. My grandparents would speak it in the house and then they'd switch over to English for us unless they were chewing us out, which they'd do in Spanish.

The Equivocal Latino dynamic can also be circumstantial, playing out in the workplace but not in personal lives. Equivocal Latinos sometimes define themselves situationally and are astute about fulfilling the perceptions and expectations of others. Thus their identity is based more on their personal interactions than their Latino background. Darren explains:

> Personally, I think of myself as being Mexican, but professionally, I don't wear that on my sleeve. And it's not because of anything that I'm ashamed of or don't want to talk about; I just never wanted to stress that identity as if I was looking for something. I didn't want any special treatment.

Frankly, I view myself as an American first, and I think the great thing about being an American versus being of any other country is that you can have two identities as an American: American and Mexican. I can do both and can be proud of both because that's what we do in America. We embrace our heritage because we're a melting pot, people coming from everywhere.

My background is an important part of my life personally, but when I'm at work, I just am who I am. From time to time my being Mexican comes up, of course. I'm there to support, but I don't lead with my ethnicity.

I've mentored people over the years, and they ask, "How did you get where you are?" I always tell people, "Just focus on getting results. Don't focus on your heritage as part of your job." I worry that my being Mexican may be used as a reason for a handout. I agree that your heritage is who you are, and I wouldn't shy away from it. But it's difficult to argue with results.

In a conversation Andrés had with his colleague Jorge Farías, a senior client partner at Korn Ferry, he sounded a bit wistful about the choices he had made considering the pressures in his career:

I remember what it was like during the times right after affirmative action, immediately following the groundbreaking civil rights movement, and well into the 1990s. It felt to me as though many companies and industries still did not view people of color as equally intelligent as those of the dominant culture.

My internal voice told me to just do the best job in whatever situation I found myself. I naively believed it would be hard for people to deny me what I deserved if I performed at high levels. I trusted my inner voice but still worried about external and unknown factors that could hinder my development, my progress, and my success.

To this day, I wonder if my lighter skin, my intense focus on education (earning a doctorate), and my working hard to avoid any hint of an accent—in effect, my efforts at assimilation—weren't ultimately the key that opened doors for me. But I do wonder at what cost to me personally.

The Retro Latino

It is possible for some individuals to maintain an orientation throughout their lives with little or no movement or change. But life as an Equivocal Latino is not predetermined as something people have to stay with if they do not want to. Latinos constantly make choices about how they see their difference and how they accommodate societal messages about themselves.

This happens regardless of whether there had or had not been much Latino cultural influence during the formative years. Ultimately cultural identity is a lot about choice.

The Retro Latino goes to great lengths to reconnect, rediscover, or discover those roots for the first time. They end up taking Spanish, learning how to dance salsa, bachata, or reggaeton. They start reading Latin American literature and begin hanging out with more Latinos or joining Latino organizations for the first time.

Others even start to date Latinas or Latinos, something they had never done before.

A few stories:

Jorge Figueredo, retired executive vice president of HR at McKesson Corporation, was born in Cuba.

When his young parents immigrated to Union City, New Jersey (a place with many Hispanic families) and then to Harrington Park, New Jersey (overwhelmingly Anglo), he did not speak for a while as a child because he was confused as to which language to use.

There were several scuffles when some of the local kids on the streets made fun of him. This mistreatment continued all through middle school, with a few locals making it clear they didn't appreciate having a Latino in their community.

> Due to these experiences with being different, before college I had always stressed my Americanism and tried to suppress my Cuban identity. But I had an awakening regarding my Latino-ness at Fairfield University, a Jesuit institution in Connecticut. Suddenly there were more Latinos as I met students from Puerto Rico, Cuba, and other parts of Latin America. I took a course in Latin American studies at the urging of a Cuban professor who was also a Castro sympathizer.
>
> In fact, I began to realize that I *was* different in trivial as well as more profound ways. For example, growing up we were always late for things when my mom took me because she had a different perspective on being "on time" versus being "late." Also,

my parents would have a big party each year, and
my large extended family eventually became a part
of the social fabric in my childhood community.
Further, politics was always a topic debated passionately in the house.

My parents were worried that America was changing for the worse due to drugs and the sexual revolution. In addition, my college education led me to
have some intense political debates with my dad,
an exile from Castro's Cuba. But I also had debates
with my Marxist professor. I saw myself as less ideo-
logical and more pragmatic.

Emblematically, how he manages his name is a full fusion of
this complex dual identity. He never changed the spelling to
"George," yet he introduces himself to others with the English
pronunciation.

Yvonne Garcia, chief of staff to the chairman and CEO for State
Street Corporation, started her Retro Latina journey as a teenager
and fully realized the process in her twenties. But in contrast to Jorge,
she took the Latina identity further.

As I was growing up, I wondered if it was okay
to be Hispanic. Perhaps there was an underlying
force within me that taught me not to highlight
it as much (maybe it was just survival skills) so I
could just fit into an all-White school. I think I had
learned this behavior of, "OK, cool, your last name
is Garcia and you're Dominican, but maybe you
don't need to promote it as much."

Being Latina probably didn't become a cool thing
to me until mid–high school years where I started to

meet other Hispanics and other women who were like me.

Then I moved from the underlying notion of "I'm Latina but the world doesn't need to know; they'll figure it out," to now as an adult I'm the opposite: I lead with the fact that I'm Latina.

These complex dynamics of identity manifested themselves not just for many of the executives but also for many of the young professionals in our focus groups.

Here are the comments of a Latina, a professional in the finance industry from our USC focus group:

> I work in Newport Beach, a California community that is predominantly Anglo. So, my attitude was more of a hide your Latino-ness, tone it down because when you go to these events there are C-level people and senior vice presidents and your top Ivy League, typical White-person-with-money crowd.
>
> I totally figured out their culture and their norms and modified my way of speaking to people. But the cost was that I couldn't be myself, be authentic.
>
> It took me being in the Latina Leadership Academy at USC to start to own who I was, own my Latina-ness, own my culture, and really relate to people as fully myself as I embraced my culture and became authentic. Because the more you hide your Latina-ness, the more you're not being yourself. You can't be as successful as you want to be when you're not being authentic because you're hiding who you really are.

> For me it has always been challenging to be the
> Latina that I am, but then as I accepted who I was
> and accepted my Latina-ness, I started to brand my-
> self around it. Now people know who I am. When
> people ask me what my name is, I say "Janet *Perez*."
> You'll never hear me just say "I'm Janet." No, "I'm
> Janet Perez." "Do you speak Spanish?" "Yes, I speak
> Spanish." I learned to embrace who I really am be-
> cause when I was walking into these huge network-
> ing events, I would just be in a corner by myself.
> When I accepted who I was, that's when I became
> more confident, surer of my identity.

Keep in mind that some Retro Latinos may not have been fully exposed to their Latino background, history, or culture during their childhood. But as individuals mature and change their surroundings, the lens with which they view their Latino-ness may widen.

Several of the leaders we interviewed who grew up in mostly European-American environments had their Latino identity awakened when they moved to a place where there were more Latinos or where Latinos made the effort to find each other and network.

When this happens, feelings of isolation are more easily pushed aside by the simple presence of and interaction with other Latinos. In the myriad Latino affinity settings of employee resource groups and professional associations that Robert has operated in, he frequently hears from many Latinos of how refreshing it is for them to see so many Latinos who are extremely proud of their Hispanic heritage and who wear their Latino identity as a badge of pride.

In many, this pride awakens a desire to let those aspects of their Latino heritage peek out, slowly at first, and incrementally revealing themselves more fully until it becomes a combination of a cultural identity blossoming from within, accelerated by increasing the number of Latino culture inputs, leading to an identity metamorphosis.

The Invisible Latino

The Invisible Latinos are the ones who ignore or even disown their Latino heritage, often won't even acknowledge that they speak Spanish, don't want their parents to come visit them, or just pretend to be as White as their college friends or workmates even though they did grow up with a Latino experience.

They prefer to identify themselves and others as "just people," and claim to be color-blind because of their preference to view each person as distinct from their ethnic or racial background. Juan Galarraga, another Unapologetic Latino, also must fight the temptation not to judge:

> As you go higher and higher in organizations, I've seen some Latino leaders almost forget that they're Latino. I don't know if it's the pressure of fitting in.

Juan goes further and indicates that rather than giving in to that peer pressure to fit in, he actually embraces being different:

> When people make fun of my accent, I cannot be prouder of my accent. After all, I know who I am, and I stay grounded by understanding what's impor-tant in life and by not forgetting where I came from.

Some Latinos who may have more Anglo features, such as blond hair and blue eyes, may choose to connect more closely with their European-American features and all that is connoted by them over their Hispanic heritage. They see their Whiteness as the essential and primary element of their identity and view the world through a White-tinted lens. Invisible Latinos also tend to view the shortage of Latinos in senior roles as the result of individual failure and not as bias or discrimination against Latinos.

Consider the Latino or Latina who hears about some Latino professional organization and says, "You know what, I don't want to get involved." We asked Victor Arias how he would respond:

> I can be a little judgmental when people tell me that. However, I have to think about what stage in their life they're at. When I see young Latinos who are just making their way into corporate America, I say, "The most important thing you need to do is to be extremely successful at your job." That may take a toll timewise on their involvement in the community, so I tend to give them a pass and support them building an incredible reputation in whatever role they're trying to pursue. But where I am less understanding is with those that have clearly done well. If they are not giving back, it tells me that, one, they don't care about the community, and two, there are some real insecurities about being perceived as Latino. I tell them, "You've been to college. Do you think you're the exception to the rule?" "Oh yeah," they say, "we're very fortunate." I say, "You've been given a lot, and it might be good to think about helping others, don't you think?"

The fact that none of the executives we interviewed disowned their Latino identity tells us that one dimension to strong leadership is authenticity. We believe it's no coincidence that these individuals are successful leaders and that they never gave up and disowned their heritage.

Don't get us wrong. Invisible Latinos can attain success, but this book is a *Latino* executive manifesto, not just an executive manifesto. The invisible ones may be executives, but they're not *Latino* executives; they've disowned that part. They're not *manifesting*. This book is the manifesto of leaders who are successful and who definitely embrace their Latino-ness.

This journey into Latino-ness is not only about inner individual identity work as we have seen in this chapter; it also demands outer communal identity work—defining who we are as a Latino community in the U.S. And here we have a lot of work to do, as we will see in the next chapter, "Intra-Latino Divides: Truth or Consequences."

CHAPTER 3

Intra-Latino Divides:
Truth or Consequences

La cultura consiste en conexiones, no de separaciones:
especializarse es aislar.

Culture consists of connections, not of separations:
to specialize is to isolate.

—Carlos Fuentes, *Myself with Others: Selected Essays*

Previously we delved into the dynamics of cultural identity crisis and resolution through the lens of the individual. But cultural identity must also be seen through a group identity perspective. Who do Latinos say we are collectively? Suddenly a simple question gets complex.

Now we must look at a more negative view as we explore the shadow side of Latino reality in the U.S. We will eventually delve into the inspiring and uplifting Latino story, which includes a rising pan-Latino consciousness unfolding in corporate America and in

53

the country as a whole. First, however, we need to acknowledge the barriers we ourselves create that further complicate the obstacles we find in corporate America.

Elements that divide us include our nationality, our socioeconomic and racial backgrounds (whether or not one grew up in the U.S.), and the languages we speak as well as the accents we may retain.

Nationalistic Divides

There is vast diversity beneath that umbrella labeled "Latino," because Latinos can be economic or political refugees, or both. Others are descendants of families who lived in the part of Mexico that was annexed by the U.S. in the Mexican-American War. In addition to the immigrant waves of first-, second-, third-, and fourth-generation Latinos, other Latinos include the Spanish-, English-, and Spanglish-dominants, the millennial, Gen Xer, and boomer Latinos, and the racial spectrum of White, Indigenous, Black, and Asian, as well as the twenty-seven different nationalities that being Latino comprises.

In the U.S., the most divisive differences among Latinos are the ones around national heritage. While this may seem to be a harmless issue, and even fun when it comes to World Cup favorites and bragging rights, these nationalistic fissures are the most debilitating in terms of Latinos gaining collective power commensurate to their rising numbers.

This phenomenon arises in part when Latinos view themselves primarily in terms of their nationality and do not necessarily identify with Latinos of all other nationalities. Having great pride in one's own nationality and viewing it positively is not wrong or destructive. But as Ferdman and Gallegos point out,[1] it does create a problem when these individuals identify themselves exclusively with their country of origin and view Latinos from other nationalities as deficient or inferior. This inevitably leads to a more narrow and exclusive view of their Latino identity.

Until Latinos can collectively and cohesively address this dimension of Latino identity, they will be responsible for their lack of advancement. The nationality differences have become more fissures than features. George Herrera, owner of Herrera-Cristina Group, describes it this way:

> When growing up in New York City, we had no issue across the different Latino groups. It was a true melting pot; you had Puerto Ricans, Cubans, Dominicans, Peruvians, Chicanos, and we just got along.
>
> But when I got to the U.S. Hispanic Chamber of Commerce in 1998, I saw the underpinnings of what was keeping the Hispanic community down in America—an ethnic turf. The feeling was that there was no way a Mexican in L.A. was going to let a Puerto Rican out of New York be a spokesperson for them. "Hold on a second," was my response. "We're talking about an economic development agenda, and so what are you guys fighting over? If anything, you are fighting over the crumbs anyway because you're being nickeled and dimed by White America."

Forcepoint Chief Strategy and Trust Officer Myrna Soto agrees:

> I often think about our broader Hispanic community, and how we often hurt each other because of our sub-cultures. The Mexicans versus the Cubans versus the Venezuelans versus the Colombians. I think about the power we have as a collective. And

for some reason, there are these subcultures that create diminishing returns for our advancement.

Socioeconomic Divides

Socioeconomic differences often accompany the national identities divide. Cubans who fled the island during Castro's revolution have a higher per capita income than Mexicans and Central Americans, causing some elitist attitudes. Puerto Ricans are U.S. citizens by birth and sometimes have a condescending attitude toward Mexicans and others whose parents, or they themselves, are here undocumented. Another factor is the classic *us versus them* dynamic that develops to allow groups of people to judge and negatively stereotype other groups. Thus Latinos fall prey to the very forms of discrimination they themselves face in White corporate America.

The Latino community also carries a legacy of classism that is more powerful than racism in Latin culture. For example, Myrna talks about living in the Miami area:

> If you were fortunate enough to live in Coral Gables, you were viewed as a little higher up in the class. Those who lived there saw themselves as more refined, with a little bit more panache and prestige. Hialeah, on the other hand, where I grew up, was more blue collar, grassroots, working class. And those distinctions held as Latinos across Miami interacted with one another.

The former AT&T executive Patricia Diaz Dennis experienced this as the child of an expat when they lived in Santiago, Chile:

> There were a couple of guys I dated while in high school who just stopped dating me because I wasn't

wealthy, which they had assumed I was because we had come from the U.S. But once they came to our home, saw where we lived, they realized I wasn't what they viewed as the typical American. I was brown-haired and darker skinned like they were. I remember when one of them broke up with me, he told me about his earlier girlfriend who had a big house; her father was an officer in some big American company. I felt so powerless because I was being judged by things I could not control.

Racial Divides

Latinos can also carry biases against people of different races. As a people we have not been exempt from expressions of racism toward those with darker skin or Asian physical features, either within or outside of our own communities.

Facing up to our own racial prejudices can be difficult because many of us have been on the receiving end of discrimination. We may bristle at the idea that racism may be present within our culture. However, there is an unmistakable pattern in our Latino communities: the darker one's skin, the less favored one may be in the eyes of the public, employers, and even family members. The stories are plentiful of lighter-skinned siblings faring better than their darker-skinned kin.

In Latin American countries where almost everyone is ethnically Latino, the visuals are stark. Those who are darkest skinned tend to be lower on the socioeconomic ladder. In Brazil, which is about 50 percent Black or mixed race, or in Colombia, where that figure is 25 percent, there is a near-zero Black Latino representation among executives, senior leaders, and managers. Even at corporate diversity conferences in these countries, the highly committed participants from major corporations have a hard time assembling racial diversity, even in token ways.

Across Latin American countries, myriad varieties of deprecatory statements about those with darker skin tones can be heard.

In the U.S. this legacy shows up in underlying racial tensions between Latinos and African-Americans. It's a complicated dynamic, since, as we have seen, many Latinos are also Black racially. But lighter-skinned Latinos often must recognize their own unconscious racial biases toward Afro-Latinos, Afro-Americans, Afro-Caribbeans, and Africans. These interactions are further complicated by an economic system that often pits Latinos and Blacks against each other for low-paying jobs.

Racial tensions don't surge just among these different people of color. They can also show up in negative attitudes toward European-Americans that can then spill over into judging fellow Latinos and Latinas for their associations with them. "I was criticized for marrying an Anglo by a Chicano law student in an article in the La Raza newsletter," shares Patricia Diaz Dennis. She elaborates:

> One guy wrote an article about amphibians that are "...neither at home at land or sea. They adopt White man's ways, they take a White man's side, they marry White men."

Spanish-Language and Accent Divides

Latinos can also be judged by other Latinos for their accented Spanish or English, or for not speaking Spanish at all. Victor Arias of Diversified Search shares this story:

> When I was working at the bank in Houston, my accounts were all in Mexico. So I used to go to Mexico,

but my Spanish wasn't very good and it veered more toward Spanglish. I remember one of the first meetings I had with a client in Monterrey. The guy says, *"¿De donde eres?"* (Where are you from?) I said, "El Paso." He said, "Aaah," like, *OK, I get it now.* That embarrassed and hurt me. They thought less of me because I was not from Mexico. I developed this insecurity about that.

So I went back and learned Spanish really well. A few months later, I was back down there with other clients and I get that question again, *"¿De donde eres?"* *"Norte, buey,"* (from the North), which I chased with some Mexican slang. In fact, I had started to use *"buey"* a lot. This time I got a different kind of "Aaah." I now had a different kind of acceptance there.

Accents and language are indeed heartfelt and important topics to many Latinos in defining their cultural identity. After a successful diversity conference a few years ago, Andrés was at a dinner in Boston's North End, at the outdoor patio of Ristorante Fiore, an Italian restaurant on Hanover Street. A group of Latinos—some sipping wine, others espresso, between bites of bruschetta and raw oysters—began discussing and debating the role of accented English as it related to Latino identity in the workplace.

As the alcohol and caffeine took their effect, the conversation about how we sound dipped into a discussion about identity and success for minorities. Why it is that having a French or British accent is seen as a plus, but having a Spanish accent a minus? And because of this, should Latinos who speak English with a Spanish accent work at reducing their accent?

The answers were not easy, the implications uncomfortable. Here we are, a table of Latinos from different countries and with different migration stories, each having made different choices.

What path should each of us take? One person described visits to the U.S. when he was young; with his heavily accented English, he faced ridicule and teasing at best, discrimination at worst. This experience motivated him to work on losing his Spanish accent when he came to this country for college.

As he calibrated his inflections, pitches, and tones, the change in responses to his words clearly shifted toward more positive reactions. From that point on, it became clear to him that many English-dominant Euro-Americans heavily weighed their value assessment of words spoken by Spanish-dominant speakers according to the density of their accent.

But others around the table at Ristorante Fiore had made different choices, equally valid. How they sound, including their accented English, is part of their Latino identity. It is a marker of who they are culturally in the same way that rolling one's r's or pronouncing Martínez, Ochoa, Jimenez, and Castillo in the original Spanish rather than in American English are language markers of a Latino identity so paramount that even when they could use the more Anglicized name, they don't. Others choose to always use the more Anglicized names.

Grew Up in Latin America versus Grew Up in the U.S.

One of the most apparent divides left unspoken is the sense that Latinos who grew up in Latin America may, in relation to Latinos who grew up in the U.S., enjoy preferential treatment from corporate America when companies seek to increase their Latino diversity.

While we have not been able to track down comparative statistics, this is spoken more in whispers than in pronouncements from the stage: observations are often made that the Latino executives being extolled by companies as evidence of their commitment to diversity are not Hispanic Americans, but rather Latin Americans. While this was not true from our sample of executives for this book (thirteen of the twenty were born in the U.S.), the perception is real and creates underlying unrest.

What could be contributing to the possibility of preferential treatment? A few thoughts:

- Latin American–born professionals who immigrate to the U.S. often have a socioeconomic advantage in that they are more likely to have been raised in middle-class or even upper-class environments than many Hispanic Americans, whose small town or rural immigrant parents may have started with less education and fewer resources.
- These Latin American elites often have easier access to networks within the U.S. Through cocktail parties, dinners, and business conferences, these networks provide opportunities for seamless acculturation to corporate American ways and access to a greater number of career opportunities.
- Latin American–born Latinos often feel they can't relate to Hispanic American Latinos who grew up in, or in close proximity to, mainstream American culture, to the extent that many of them don't even speak Spanish. The Latin Americans struggle to understand how this can be possible.
- Because those raised in Latin America read and write Spanish as their primary language, they are better able to take advantage of opportunities that require Spanish fluency, thus giving them access to more opportunities.

- Conversely, Hispanic Americans perceive that the Latin Americans are not tuned in to the realities of being Latino in the U.S.—that they have a rarefied view of American life that is far removed from East L.A., the Bronx, or San Antonio.

- Some of the executive roles available in corporations that make it a priority to seek out Latino talent are for Latin American operations; these corporations assume that those from the area will have an advantage in having connections and knowing the region, compared to those born in the U.S.

Overcoming the Divides

There are still obstacles to a greater sense of common purpose and unity among Latinos. However, there is also Latino unity, and the Latino experience in the U.S. is replete with powerful stories to prove it. Some of that unity has always existed, as illustrated in the stories of many of our executives who came from pan-Latino, multiethnic Latino enclaves and who joined organizations representing that unity. Some of this cohesiveness is new, as Latinos begin to connect with the reality that their growing numbers will translate into greater power and influence only if there is greater sense of common purpose. This sense has also accelerated as the anti-immigrant and anti-Latino walls have gone up. External threats, such as those we are experiencing as of this second edition, make those intra-Latino fissures trivial in comparison to what is truly an existential threat from rising xenophobia against people that don't look like White America. Victor Arias describes when his sense of identity sharpened:

> When I moved to Chicago, that's where I think the true Latino-ness really started, because that's when I ran into second, third generations—whether they were Puerto Ricans, Mexicans, Salvadorans—who

had sort of mixed. You had *MexiRicans* and you had *Salva Mexicans* and all these other things. My mind thought, *This is really cool, this is what is the fabric of America, what I think of as Latinos in America.* So I became much more open to seeing Latinos as a much larger group than just my own Mexican-American experience.

And Patricia Diaz Dennis explains:

We shouldn't be asking, "How American are you or how Latino are you?" All of us are unique individuals; there should be no litmus test. People feel self-conscious if they don't speak Spanish well. My mother keeps telling me I sound like a gringa.

The driver at one of the companies on whose board I serve is from Puerto Rico, and he said to me, "I can't tell you how proud I am you're on this board. I can't tell you what it means to me." I cried. When I leave that board, he's going to be one of the people I go to dinner with. Because they are brethren—or sisters—right? It's really critical to me to not forget where you're from.

Authenticity really matters. How do I want to feel with a group of Latinos? I want all of us to be authentic with each other and not pretend to be something we aren't. I was born in this country, so of course I'm going to sound a little different. I came from New Mexico, but I also think that we are helping each other whether we speak Spanish or not.

The Power of an Integrated Cultural Identity

Latinos are a bicultural people. In his book *The Hispanic Condition,*[2] Ilan Stavans describes the concept of Latino identity as being almost like a labyrinth because of its maze-like qualities. For some Latinos, trying to find their way through this labyrinth is frustrating and exasperating because it can be curved, distorted, wandering, and complex. This may help us understand why these Latinos chose to reject this chaotic Latino identity situation because of its tendency to infuriate, confuse, and disorient them.

Imagine the difficulty these Latinos face in trying to explain to non-Latinos why a new immigrant from Venezuela shouldn't be assumed to have the same exact needs as a fourth-generation Chicano or a Manhattan-born Latino with Newyorican parents. When we make that assumption, we can begin to grasp why they chose not to deal with the issue of Latino identity altogether.

Others choose to face the cultural dilemma head on, weighing how much they want to identify with their ethnic roots versus how much they want to embrace mainstream American culture as the core of who they are.

The Latino executives featured in this book, for the most part, learned not to view this tension as an either/or dilemma but as a both/and celebration. Their key to not being lost in the cultural identity maze is *to embrace a bicultural identity*.

The Unapologetic Latinos tell stories of how they skillfully modulate their Latino selves, cross-culturally adapting to those who don't share their same cultural heritage. Equivocal Latinos, who often become Retro Latinos, embrace their lost or weakened heritage with more enthusiasm.

This is how many Latino executives become bicultural, fully embracing their Latino heritage whether it was always there or blossomed later in life. At the same time, they successfully and smoothly operate within the norms of corporate America. It's a duality they all manage. Victor attributes his Latino upbringing to broadening his view of other cultures:

> My upbringing was very rooted in respecting people from all walks of life. That's who I am. I'm very proud of being American, and I'm very proud of being Latino. I can value other cultures even though I'm American and Latino. I love to talk about other cultures, languages. Key experiences in both cultures really shaped me, and I learned how to bob and weave. And that's when I felt I belong here in the corporate world. Nobody's going to tell me I don't belong.

Latinos in the U.S. are a multistage, multiethnic, multiage phenomenon. The Super Bowl and La Copa Mundial (World Cup). McDonald's and *arroz con gandules* (rice and pigeon peas). *American Idol* and *telenovelas*. The American Dream and *la patria de mis padres* (the country of my parents). No surprise, then, that according to Pew Hispanic Research, seven in ten young Hispanics report that they regularly blend English and Spanish into a Spanglish hybrid.[3] These young Latinos epitomize the new Latino-American multidimensional identity.

In fact, half of Latinos in the U.S. are English-dominant millennials who, paradoxically, also tend to identify with their parents' country of origin (Colombia, Costa Rica, Argentina, and so on).

Latino talent, like the leaders interviewed for this book, embodies these multidimensional characteristics. Fully both bicultural and tricultural, they identify equally with their Latino and mainstream American selves. Their patter often flows back and forth between

English and Spanish. Even in business conversations in English with other Latinos, Spanish expressions provide color commentary. Their stories of not fitting in live side by side with stories of professional success in spite of the odds they've overcome.

Many Latinos actually straddle the fusion of more than two identities. Millennial Latinos are more likely to come from mixed ethnic and racial backgrounds, and they self-identify with the blended identities of Blaxican, Mexipino, or China-Latina. Plus, the creative tension caused by the generational diversity of boomers, Gen X, millennials, and Gen Z when they interact with each other also shows up in Latino communities.

Further, that same Pew study found that only 16 percent of millennial Latinos see themselves as White, compared to twice as many older Latinos. This means that they are less likely to be assimilationist mind-set than were their first-generation parents who, as they faced discrimination due to their limited or accented English, chose not to teach their children Spanish.

We pick our cultural identity spots. *Este es quien soy* (This is who I am). Increasingly for more Latinos, particularly Latino millennials, the assimilation survival tactics of their parents are not as necessary or desirable. Their modern path forward has been to embrace both the Latino and mainstream American culture. It's biculturalism.

Given all this variety, Latino identity cuts across a wide spectrum of choices of how much of that identity to embrace. This spectrum can range from the fiercely nationalistic to the fully assimilated into mainstream American culture.

Indeed, the range of choices of how to express their Latino selves in American society are as diverse as the people who make up the Latino/Hispanic fabric *en los Estados Unidos de America*.

Whether one is an Unaware Equivocal, a Consciously Aware Equivocal, a Retro, or an Unapologetic Latino, cultural identity is a choice.

The successful Latinos we have chosen to highlight have taken into account the benefits of not only embracing their Latino identity but also letting others know they identify as Latinos. They have been able to both successfully educate others about racial and ethnic diversity, as well as challenge prevailing stereotypes about Latinos held by others.

This biculturality—this tighter embrace of Latino identity we see in the executives and in the Gen X and millennial generations—sets the stage for conflict with some of the key cultural markers and preferences of corporate America.

What are these cultural tensions, how have successful Latino executives navigated them, and where does corporate America need to make adjustments if it's going shed its shame of having only 5 percent of the Hispanic workforce in executive officer positions in Fortune 500 firms? We'll turn our attention to this conflict next.

CHAPTER 4

Culture Clash: Can Corporate and Latino Cultures Be Reconciled?

La preservación de la propia cultura no requiere desprecio o falta de respeto hacia otras culturas.

Preservation of one's own culture does not require contempt or disrespect for other cultures.

—César Chávez, American labor activist

Herein is the conundrum: corporate America says it wants more Latino managers and leaders. Young Latino professionals in growing numbers aspire to this leadership. Yet, as we have seen so far, what should be mutually reinforcing trends to speed up advancement are instead two forces increasingly in conflict due to deep differences between corporate culture and Latino culture.

If businesses are to overcome the 5 percent shame, they must go beyond the necessary public declarations in support of diversity and take a zero-tolerance stance toward overt bias. This requires facing up to unconscious cultural biases that can negatively affect the evaluation of both the performance and the potential of Latino talent and generate work environments that are unattractive to many Latinos. Corporations should become more conscious of Latinos' demands that they demonstrate for greater cross-cultural agility. Doing so will require the following:

- Gaining a deep understanding of the archetypical cultural preferences of Latinos
- Nurturing self-awareness of the current cultural preferences of the corporation
- Determining how to bridge the gap in a mutually reciprocal way

Latino Cultural Preferences and How They Compare to Corporate Culture

Often, when Latinos have graduated from college and gain their first corporate job, the signs that their past experiences haven't adequately prepared them for the prevailing corporate culture job that can be in such contrast to Latino culture. The trivial becomes precursor to much more profound differences. Charlie Garcia, former CEO of Sterling Financial Group and current CEO of Tendrel, grew up in Panama. He tells this story:

> My first roommate at the Academy was trying to break the ice by telling me a joke about *Mork and Mindy*. I innocently asked, "Who's Mork and Mindy?" He replied, "What planet did you get off of?" Later I would put my salsa music on in the weekend and people would knock on the door yelling, "Turn that s*** off. We're in the United States."

> Then somebody changed my nametag from Garcia
> to O'Garcia, and they started calling me Ogarsha
> because they said I looked Irish.

The differences are cultural as well as socioeconomic. Patricia
Diaz Dennis tells of the time peer lawyers were talking about taking a ski trip:

> And then I said to the person next to me, "So
> where do you go to rent skis?" He just looked at
> me and said, "Oh, no need, I *own* mine." I had no
> idea that this was even possible.

While these more surface differences are fairly innocent and can
lead to entertaining cocktail reception conversation, they are
just the tip of the iceberg of differences in cultural values and
assumptions that lie deep below the surface of polite interactions.
Clueless assumptions lead to the unconscious biases by individuals in the dominant culture, and those biases get codified in talent management systems (leadership competencies, development
programs, performance assessment, high-potential identification)
in ways that systematically reinforce the glass ceiling for Latinos.

Dismantling these bias reinforcement mechanisms requires a grasp
of the cultural differences between mainstream corporate culture
and Latino culture.

Before elaborating on this, let's provide a primer on how to talk
about culture comparisons. We are going to compare *archetypes*,
the general tendency of a particular group to behave in certain
ways, without falling into *stereotypes*, the assumption that every
member of that group behaves according to the archetype.

Sociologists and interculturalists specialize in the study of what
happens when people from different cultures come into contact

with one another. They have been able to trace the normative, bell curve behavior of groups, fully recognizing that there are many who, for a variety of reasons, do not adhere to these norms. However, understanding the group norms is helpful in ferreting out patterns that could be in conflict and could keep Latinos from advancing.

CORPORATE ATTITUDES: EUROPEAN AMERICAN VERSUS HISPANIC

Locus of Control
God helps those who help themselves versus si Dios quiere (God willing)

Ascribing Status
Egalitarianism versus hierarchy

Identity
I versus we

Process
Follow the rules versus go with the flow

Managing Emotions
Stiff upper lip versus pura vida

Time Management
Clock versus event-oriented

Let's look at six cultural dimensions (taken or adapted from the various works of interculturalists Geert Hofstede,[1] Fons Trompenaars, and Charles Hampden-Turner[2] and applied to the Hispanic-American context) where these two cultures can be at odds with each other.

As we point out the differences, the question arises: whose responsibility is it to close the cultural gap? The leaders we interviewed stressed the concept of reciprocal adaptation. However, for too long the full burden has been put on Latinos to assimilate into the dominant culture. As we saw in the previous chapter, doing so can be detrimental to Latinos' own sense of personal identity and empowerment. Plus, corporations lose the benefits of the differences in perspectives and backgrounds that Latinos bring to the workplace.

There may be some cultural dimension, depending on the cultural gap, where resisting adaptation to the majority culture could be a losing battle. At the same time, there are other areas where standing our ground—and in fact, influencing the other party's adaptation to match a Latino cultural preference—might be the healthiest way to optimize personal and organizational performance.

Let's explore these cultural gaps and how Latino leaders navigated their way among the cultural tensions. There is no clear-cut right or wrong way to do this, but these Latino and Latina leaders tended to be aware of the choices in front of them.

Locus of Control: God Helps Those Who Help Themselves versus *Si Dios Quiere* (God Willing)

Different cultures have their own beliefs about whether they can control the environment around them. *Internal control* cultures believe they have that control, whereas *external control* cultures believe they do not. European-American culture, and by extension corporate America, tends to believe the former, while Hispanic American culture believes the latter.

The belief that a person's destiny, their path in life, is determined by God is the mind-set of fatalism. Such a belief leads many Latinos to have a yielding view of life, and thus prepare themselves to consent to God's predetermined fate for them. A

2002 study conducted by the Pew Hispanic Center[3] shows how prevalent this feeling is in the Latino community: 53 percent of Latinos in the U.S. agreed that it doesn't do any good to plan for the future because one has no control over it. Patricia Diaz Dennis explains a behavioral outcome of this *si Dios quiere* passivity: "Many of us, rather than volunteering to take on a new assignment or role, instead wait to be invited."

Cari Dominguez, former Bank of America executive and former chair of the U.S. Equal Opportunity Commission, explains how this difference can play out for a good number of Latinos wanting to climb the career ladder:

> While Anglo-Americans may believe that one can dominate the environment and external circumstances, Latinos often believe that it is not up to us, that things may be out of our hands, out of our control. This can lead to behaviors embedded in our different cultural consciousness such as "toot your own horn" versus "humbly wait to be noticed." Many of us Latinos have a hard time tooting our own horns, but it is a behavior that is necessary to get ahead in corporate America. Instead we hold on tightly to lessons from *mamá* to not be proud, not call attention to our accomplishments, but instead allow others to point them out. So as we look at this cultural gap, we need to realize that we can't be culturally bound and wait for somebody to do something on our behalf. We need to do a better job of marketing ourselves and touting our accomplishments.

In our research sample, we did notice that there was also a gender dimension to this cultural dynamic. While both Latinos and

Latinas wrestled with this similar upbringing acculturation, it was clearly more deeply rooted, and therefore more of an articulated struggle, for the women. For example, Lisa Garcia Quiroz, the former senior vice president for Time Warner, struggled with the religious aspect of our culture. She explains:

> I think that the disadvantage, and I hate to call it a disadvantage, in our culture is that we value humility so it's not in our DNA to brag about ourselves. It's a very Catholic thing, right? The meek shall inherit the earth.

Former vice president of General Motors Grace Lieblein layers on another behavior that stems from this lack of competitiveness:

> I am one of the least competitive people I know. It's probably to a detriment, frankly, but it's just not in me. Life to me is "What you see is what you get," and I'd just as soon help the person who's next to me than push him off the ladder. Sometimes that worked, and sometimes I probably didn't get as far as I could've if I'd been more competitive. But I'd rather be myself than be somebody else and get higher in the organization.

Corporate American culture, on the other hand, is premised on leaders, managers, and employees taking more entrepreneurial initiative within the corporate structure, whether providing innovative ideas or taking charge of their own careers.

The rallying cry of "You own your own career," while making complete sense as a default belief for the majority culture, feels foreign to many Latinos and can actually be disengaging and even marginalizing. Many Latinos are reluctant to ask for things they want and need.

But "owning your career" may be one rule of the road that is difficult to buck if Latinos seek to succeed in corporate America. Many of the executives we interviewed had to learn to speak up for themselves, and doing so is one of the first principles these leaders teach other up-and-coming Latinos. We further explain how they accomplished this speaking up for themselves in chapter 6, where representative leaders explain how to see ambition as honorable.

Ascribing Status: Hierarchy versus Egalitarianism

Latinos can tend to be hierarchical compared to the egalitarian European-American approach. This tendency can cut both ways in terms of emerging Latino talent either engaging more senior leaders too deferentially, without sufficient assertiveness, or Latino leaders acting with too much forcefulness as they gain positional authority.

The historical, religious, and anthropological roots of these two very different views of status go back to Reformation times in the Middle Ages and colonial times in both British and Spanish colonies in the Americas.

Martin Luther's Protestant Reformation was a direct challenge to the Roman Catholic Church's interpretation of divine hierarchy, which vested the priests with the power of being the only ones through which the faithful could connect with God. Luther's theology of the "priesthood of all believers" was enabled by the disruptive technology of that time—the printing press—which put German-language Bibles in the hands of the laity, thereby democratizing access to God.

As Catholicism made its way south and Protestantism north, the Spanish colonies were conquered by soldiers under a full top-down military structure. In contrast, the British colonies were settled by families fleeing religious persecution. While the racism of the British settlers resulted in near annihilation of the Indigenous people—who suffered also at the hands of the racist Spanish *conquistadores*—the colonizers' in-group values played out very differently when it came to more Protestant egalitarian processes and structures. In contrast, the Spanish colonizers engrained their military and Catholic-influenced hierarchical structures into most aspects of Latin American society.

Fast-forward to the twenty-first century, and these long-ago legacies still have residual effects. Many Latinos grow up in strong matriarchies or patriarchies. Given the deeply held value of family and its inherently hierarchical structures, they tend to be more deferential to authority. This leads to the passivity more prevalent among Latino talent. This hierarchical view of status reinforces Latinos' common belief that not much is in their control, which in turn leads toward a sense of having less self-agency—the ability to give voice to one's aspirations, hopes, and needs.

The management practice of paternalism has a long-established history in Latin America. A key feature of paternalism is a set of benevolent management practices whereby the *patrón* (boss) provides for employees' welfare. Paternalism has been a strong force with workers because it is derived from traditional, gendered family roles and from established Catholic precepts that cast employers as caretakers of an employee family. The employment equation, then, is that employees simply have to work hard and the *patrón* will take care of them. Some Latinos still subscribe to the paternalism phenomenon and feel there is no need to call attention to their contributions or apply for promotions because their boss will automatically reward them for their hard work.

Identity: I versus We

As much as it may sound like a cliché, *familia* is exceptionally important to Latinos, but it is profoundly true, and companies chronically neglect this reality.

This all-in enveloping of *familia* in the Latino ethos comes from a sense of communal identity—*who I am is defined by whom I belong to* versus the more European-American interpretation of individualistic identity—*who I am is defined by myself.*

This too is why Latinos tend to be more group oriented when it comes to workplace dynamics. Carmen Matos, an executive at Royal Caribbean Group, put it this way in a recent conversation with one of the authors:

> We Latinos tend to be very relationship-driven, and strong relationships unleash our best selves. When we have that sense of community at work, our talent and hearts find a home. This means that quality of time spent with coworkers in the workplace versus solely what is accomplished can take on added significance. As an example, a 9 a.m. meeting in corporate America may start with a quick hello and grabbing coffee as people rush to open portfolios and get down to business. In Miami or Mexico City it will often start with warm hellos and an extended recap of weekend and family events. Then we get down to business. At the end of the day, much will have been accomplished in both worlds, but the Latino employee feels like he or she is working with colleagues who could be considered friends and extended family members. It makes for a sense of belonging at the workplace, which feeds engagement.

She adds that there was a time when this relaxed dynamic was more prevalent and valued in the U.S. before the waves of "downsizing" and "rightsizing" made the corporate picnic obsolete:

> Before that time it was easier for employees to feel like they mattered and were more than a number. But now the workplace has unfortunately become more transactional and more focused solely on getting the work done. A growing number of workers feel they must leave their hearts at home or in the parking lot. This sacrifice of culture in the workplace has been difficult for many. And it has been acutely painful for communal-oriented Latino talent.

The high value of community is not just about work-related get-togethers. It shows up in how many Latinos would prefer that workplace performance would be more about group results than individual results. There is a high sense of importance in achieving group goals, a desire to have equal distribution of regard within a group, and a strong sense of loyalty to the group. This, of course, collides with the more prevalent corporate America best practice of setting achievement and accomplishment goals and rewards at an individual level.

Community also goes a long way in explaining the Latino tendency to highly value networking, not just for socializing purposes but also to actually get things done. Like African Americans, who are also more communal, Latinos (compared to European Americans) strongly emphasize attending work- and industry-related events. It is through the relationships made and nurtured at these events that business and new career opportunities get transacted. This kind of networking is, of course, common among European Americans, but it goes into hyperdrive with many Latinos.

This communal "we" preference also affects how answers to classic interview questions can trigger unconscious biases that can be detrimental to Latino job candidates. Picture this common interview dynamic between an individualistic hiring manager and a communal Latino:

> Hiring manager: "Tell me of a time you led a team to success."
>
> Candidate: "What my *team* did was…. What my *colleagues* contributed was…. What *we* collaborated on was…"

Back in the debrief session, the hiring manager and recruiter look at each other and say:

> "I don't think that person did anything. I think he rode the backs of everyone else."
>
> Unconscious bias referee: "Really? Are you sure? Maybe it's that very kind of collaborative competency and value that our organization needs more of."

If corporate America can be more adaptive in catering to Latino communal values, it could benefit directly from more of this ethos in its midst. The American workplace's worship of the individual can be fraught with an internal competitiveness and reduced spirit of collaboration that can hinder optimizing performance.

Today's complex, hyper-interconnected, and volatile world demands fewer individualist superheroes and more group collaborators across various platforms, countries, disciplines, skills, and backgrounds. Resolving this cultural clash does not necessarily mean an *either/ or* choice, but perhaps a *both/and* approach. Bicultural Hispanic Americans often value both individual recognition and rewards based on the accomplishments of their teams.

Yvonne Garcia, chief of staff to the CEO at State Street Corporation, thinks one reason that Latina initiatives have been more prevalent of late is because companies want to build cultures that are more collaborative. She used this insight to successfully lead Latina initiatives across the country through her involvement with Association of Latino Professionals for America (ALPFA). She explains:

> From an organizational perspective, companies are starting to realize the value that women in general, and Latinas in particular, bring to the workplace: a stronger sense of collaboration to get things done, determination, perseverance—these are all traits that are highly correlated to our culture.
>
> A lot of studies have been done by Google and others that show when teams are led by women, or when there were women on the team, they tend to be more successful—for a variety of reasons. Women tend to embrace the whole team spirit more, the whole collective approach. Women aren't afraid to ask questions. So I think that companies are starting to see that the data points to high-performing teams are highly correlated with women, and in particular Latinas, being part of that.

Conversely, this sense of *familia* can become a barrier to Latino career advancement when the ties that bind hold them back from seizing opportunities that require them to move farther away from their families and communities of origin.

In the focus group we conducted in Los Angeles, several of the Latinas clearly stated they would turn down a job opportunity, even if it meant a greater title and money, if they had to move away from their families. One young Latina focus group participant said, "I'm very close to my family. That's my support system.

That's why I say no to relocation opportunities." Another young Latina added, "I would not relocate, because of my family and because I love California."

Another participant in the Chicago focus group shared how wrenching it was for her parents when she chose to move from a suburb in Chicago to downtown—just ten miles away. Since taking that step she has moved no farther, even when opportunities have presented themselves.

All the executives we interviewed who faced the choice to stay near family or move for greater opportunities did choose the latter. George Herrera, owner of the Herrera-Cristina Group, sees it this way:

> In the Latino community, we're very culturally attuned to each other, we love family, and we want to be in the family. But if you're born and raised in Miami and that opportunity is in Boise, Idaho, you'd better go.

Forcepoint executive Myrna Soto adds:

> I grew up in and spent the majority of my early adulthood in South Florida as a typical Hispanic family member where we are very enmeshed, we all live close to each other, and we don't necessarily move too far from the nest. But when the opportunity presented itself, I broke that chain by moving away.

Darren Rebelez, CEO of Casey's General Stores, explains:

> It's not a matter of whether it's right or wrong. That's always going to be a personal decision, since sometimes, depending on what's going on with the

family, it's more important to stay than to pack up and pursue another career opportunity. But you've got to recognize that the rest of the world is going to move on regardless of the decision you make.

Process: Follow the Rules versus Go with the Flow

European Americans tend to seek reassurance in the rules, whereas Latinos tend to seek redress in the particulars of each circumstance. Trompenaars and Hampden-Turner were intrigued by their research that showed how multinationals with strong corporate cultures, such as IBM, still struggled with national differences preventing their being able to work as effectively as they wanted. To better understand what was going on, they created an extensive survey with a series of "What would you do?" scenarios.

Here's one: You're riding in a car with a friend who you know is speeding. Suddenly the flashing lights of a police car appear in the rearview mirror. After pulling the car over, the officer asks you, "Was your friend speeding?" What would you answer? The answer depended on one's nationality. Ninety-seven percent of Swiss would say, "Yes, my friend was speeding," but only 32 percent of Venezuelans would give the same answer. What's going on?

The authors had come up with seven cultural dimensions to explain the different ways people from various cultures would approach the same scenarios. In the case of the speeding car, they developed a construct that identified what individual cultures determine is fair. Some cultures believe that rules apply to everyone equally. Trompenaars and Hampden-Turner referred to them as *Universalist*. Other cultures determine what is fair based on the context of the situation. They referred to these as *Particularism* cultures.

In returning to the case of the speeding ticket, you can now imagine the judgments flying. The Universalist turns to the Particularist and says, "How dare you lie to a police officer!" while the Venezuelan turns to the Swiss and retorts, "How dare you betray a friend!" Both want the same thing—fairness—but they have different ways of interpreting what fairness is. In their book the authors explain how these kinds of worldview clashes happen daily in the workplace as workers try to figure out whom to confer status to, how to get work done, and how to manage time, projects, and emotion.

Lou Nieto, former president at ConAgra's Consumer Foods, describes how he went against company rules and established protocol, following an approach that felt more appropriate to him based on his cultural lens:

> During my first year, I think it was 2005, there was a national organized labor boycott. Latinos were going to walk out of their jobs for one day in protest of how Latino immigrants were being treated and to help people understand how this country would run without Latino employees. We had fourteen manufacturing plants, three of them majority-Latino. There was a senior VP who ran manufacturing and operations and reported to me. I asked if we would be affected, and he said, "Yes, we have three locations that are primarily Latino, but we're prepared for it. First, we're telling every-one that anyone who walks out on Monday will not get paid for that day and also will get suspended for two more days without pay. In addition to that we're prepared to bring in supervisors from other plants to help cover. We will continue to operate

with a skeletal crew, but we're not going to let them shut down our plants."

And I said, "Hmm. I've got a different idea. I don't want to be punitive because these employees are part of our family and we value them." He said, "We can't just let them walk out; it sets a terrible example." I said, "We can't do it that way. What I'd like to do is tell all our plant employees, we're going to have an additional personal holiday this year, and people can choose to take it whenever they want to. Anybody who wants to take it two weeks from today when that walkout is going to occur, just let us know a week ahead of time and we'll give you this personal holiday so you can in solidarity support other Latinos across the country." He said, "What about all the non-Latinos? What happens to our plants?" I said, "Oh, they get another personal holiday also, so everybody wins. Additionally, you've got a plan to run them with a skeletal crew, but you don't have to punish anybody." He said, "OK, OK, if that's what you want." I said, "That's what I want." And we did it. Morale was so strong after that.

Coworkers addressing business issues with these contrasting worldviews are going to end up clashing regularly, which can lead to accusations dripping with moral judgments. Note that in this example, this contrast in values stems more from the primacy of relationships in Latino culture, even above the primacy of rules and processes.

In a corporate world governed by external industry, state, and federal regulations and by internal policies, this difference in cultural preferences is often difficult to reconcile—especially since many of the regulations that must be followed cannot be arbitrarily ignored without consequences for the organization. However, not all situations are governed by regulations. There are many policies or norms that can be challenged as Lou did for the sake of inclusion before the planned national organized labor boycott.

Time Management: Clock- versus Event-Oriented

What is time? Is it what is scientifically defined by the clock, with sixty seconds to the minute, sixty minutes to the hour? Or is it ruled by the circumstances of the moment? Does the meeting end at 11 a.m. on the dot because the schedule says it should, or does it go past the allotted time because the conversation in motion has not yet reached its final destination?

European Americans tend to be ruled more by the clock (referred to by interculturalists as being "clock-oriented") whereas Latinos are regulated more by the event ("event-oriented")—the former making the task at hand the top priority, the latter making the *gestalt* of the whole group most important, making them more likely to stay in the moment rather than cutting it short artificially due to what the clock says.

This is one cultural value difference for which the distance between the two narrows with each successive generation of Latinos in the U.S. As evidenced by our interviewees, those born and raised outside the U.S. who then emigrated to study and/or work tended to struggle more intensely with this divide than those Latinos who grew up in the U.S.

As mundane as the question of meeting start and end times can be, differences in the interpretation of time can be a source of great tension in the high-stakes corporate environment. Ultimately, the event-oriented Latino leaders figured out that it was a losing battle to get corporate America to be more time flexible. The stakes were too high. Having team members waiting for the one executive or leader to arrive to start a meeting had too much of a negative domino effect on productivity, because the entire organization's meetings were premised on things starting and ending on time. Their lateness showed a lack of respect for others' time.

Several of these leaders found ways to retain the value of "the moment" by recognizing when an employee needed more compassion, attention, or coaching, and giving that person the needed time, a moment that would not come back again. These leaders moved from a default of always going with the flow and the moment to qualifying those moments on a more selective basis. But their event orientation continued to serve them well in discerning the power of the moment.

Lou Nieto describes such an instance when employees needed extra attention and nurturing due to a ConAgra decision to divest a business that first needed to be turned around financially. His leadership approach, shaped by his Hispanic ethnicity, dictated a more compassionate way to handle the situation:

> The decision was made to make a public announcement about the planned divestiture. As the president of the business to be divested, I realized that it would make the turnaround incredibly difficult. Our employees in the business unit would not be motivated because they would know that they would no longer be part of ConAgra.
>
> I decided there was only one way to approach this—a way that felt right to me regardless of whether it was culturally the right thing for the corporation. So I

quickly flew to our fourteen manufacturing plants and to our corporate headquarters for that business in Chicago. I delivered the following message: "We are no longer going to be part of ConAgra. Even though we'll be a part of ConAgra for maybe two or three years, effectively we're not part of the company anymore. We're by ourselves. So I'm asking you to work really hard even though we don't know what's going to happen. I'm not asking you to do it for ConAgra, I'm asking you to do it for your family, for the people that you love and care about, whomever they may be. Because that's why you come to work. You come to work because you're working for your family, your loved ones. If you look around, the people next to you, they're doing the same thing. Now the catch is, just working really hard by yourself isn't going to help you be successful. You have to work as a team with all these other three thousand people in order for us to be successful. Because if we're not successful, it's going to affect your family." I changed the whole focus of "Let's do this one for the company." Instead it was, "Let's *not* do this one out of corporate pride, and let's *not* do this one because you're going to get big bonuses. Let's work hard because this is the only way you can provide financial security for your family." That really resonated for me culturally, and it was a message that really connected with the employees.

Managing Emotions:
Stiff Upper Lip versus *Pura Vida*

This one is fraught with the potential to stereotype and caricature. We have seen too many exaggerations on mainstream American television—from Ricky Ricardo to Sofia Vergara—that make many Latinos cringe. But it is true that the normative Latino behavior is to be more expressive than many of their European-American counterparts. Also, many Latinos have stories of being coached to "tone it down" when presenting or engaging in the corporate America context.

Myrna Soto speaks from the heart in describing this:

> There was a point in time where some of the leaders above me said, "Hey, just settle down, just because every time we have a meeting you're always kind of like…whatever." They couldn't even say the words. It made me feel bad at first. But then I defended it. "Hey, this is the way we talk; we're passionate, we talk with our hands, we're not yelling, but we're excited about something so our voice may get a little elevated."

Different interpretations of how to manage the reality of human emotions are at play here. We all have them, but Latino culture tends to value showing the emotion, while European-American culture is more about restraining the display of emotion. Like other cultural dimensions discussed, neither is right nor wrong, but they are different. In the workplace these differently interpreted behaviors can clash and lead to team dysfunction.

While most of the Latino executives we interviewed had stories of adapting to tone down their style just a bit, many found that Latino passion just kept bubbling to the surface no matter what the topic: advancing in their careers, making a difference in the world, helping raise the next generation of Latino leaders, and so on. It was this intensity that gave several of these leaders a differentiated edge in their career trajectories. Costa Ricans have a wonderful expression that captures this ethos: *pura vida* (living life fully).

For several of the interviewees, to hold back emotions or to possess that stiff upper lip seemed a technique to use in situations that would ensure effectiveness with those being addressed. But this technique could not hide the deep rivers of emotion from which they drew their inspiration—and by which they inspired others.

Monica Lozano, former CEO of ImpreMedia and CEO of College Futures Foundation, recalls having to inform employees who were going to be laid off from her family's business as one of the hardest things she has ever done, because she viewed employees as part of a family. She did so by emotionally connecting to them:

> I still choke up thinking about it. We'd made the hard decision to close the production facility and I carried the message to the company's press crews. Although we'd done everything we could to avoid layoffs and helped to place many of them in other companies, I had to tell long-term employees who'd been there more years than me in some instances, about the layoffs. I was having a hard time getting through my remarks and toward the end, one man stood up and says, "You know, *Señora Monica*, on behalf of my family I want you to know that because of you and your family, I was able to not only put food on the table, but I got my daughters through college, we own our own house and

have property in Mexico. Thanks to you and your family we have a life here, and I don't want you to forget that." That really affected me. I couldn't believe that I'm telling somebody that this was their last day at work, and he's thanking me for what we meant to him and his family.

Hired for Differences but Told to Assimilate

Some of the very actions Latinos are criticized for are those that are valued and nurtured in Latino culture. It's not acknowledged that the corporate values that are exalted and held as universal standards for how a great leader and executive should look come from the European-American context. The challenge for corporations who want to attract more Latinos is to do some soul searching about their own cultural values and realize values that often are seen as must-haves are much more subjective than the gatekeepers think they are.

Corporate America must make a distinction between true job requirements and cultural preferences that are not vital for job success. This requires self-awareness of what is preferred and why, and curiosity and education about Latino culture and its differences, as well as similarities, to corporate culture. Proactive steps must then be taken to simultaneously affirm the many dimensions of mainstream culture that have given corporate America its strength and resilience, while at the same time becoming open to new ways of growing and strengthening their companies.

These changes are not needed just so Latinos will feel more welcome and not feel they must keep sacrificing their identity at the altar of conformity. Change is also required so companies can truly benefit from the differences Latinos bring to the workplace. As demographic trends predict, the future workforce will be represented with an increasingly Latino identity, so the current unilateral approach of requiring Latinos to do all the adjusting must change.

Bottom line? Corporations need to stop saying they want to hire Latinos for their differences and subsequently coach them into assimilation by asking them to set aside those differences.

"*Al mal viento, buena cara.*"

To bad winds, a good face.

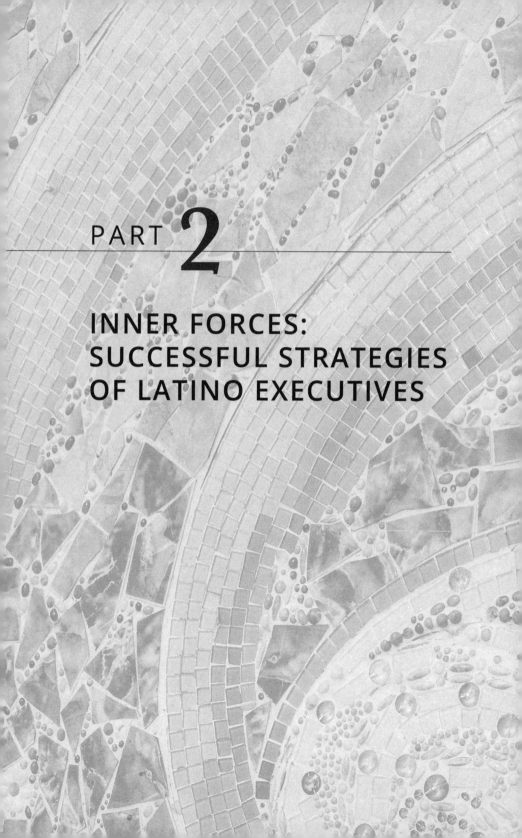

PART **2**

INNER FORCES:
SUCCESSFUL STRATEGIES
OF LATINO EXECUTIVES

In spite of the many strong, negative, and invisible forces detailed in part 1, the successful Latino executives we interviewed found ways not only to overcome the obstacles but also to thrive because of them.

Their intuitive as well as calculated strategies revolved around drawing from inner forces: optimizing educational opportunities, seeing their unique Latino backgrounds as assets, and then bearing down on mastering key leadership traits and competencies. We cover these topics in the chapters that follow.

Yet the mastery of key leadership skills does not come without challenges, such as certain Latino cultural legacies being seen as liabilities and the underlying ambivalence about power that many Latinos wrestle with—topics we explore here as well.

We wrap up part 2 by looking at how the leadership lessons learned by the Latino executives converge and diverge from the early- and mid-career experiences of Latinos.

CHAPTER 5

Reaching Outward: Education at All Costs

Hasta que tengamos igualdad en la educación, no tendremos una sociedad igualitaria.

Until we get equality in education, we won't have an equal society.

—Sonia Sotomayor, U.S. Supreme Court Justice

One overarching commonality the successful Latino executives we interviewed have had is a college education, many at a graduate level. For most, this achievement was not a given. Several were the first in their families ever to go college. The odds were against their entering college, but even more so, against their graduating with a degree in hand.

Here's what the odds would have been for them today; these odds were worse when the executives we interviewed began their journeys. If you begin with a hundred Latino freshmen in an urban public high school, twelve will drop out before graduating. Of the eighty-eight who do finish high school, only thirty-five will go on to a two- or four-year college; the other forty-nine will have entered the job market instead of furthering their education. Those forty-nine might work as mechanics, hotel housekeepers, waiters, salespeople, landscapers, storekeepers, or teachers' aides. Some may succeed financially, but most will live paycheck-to-paycheck. The thirty-five who do go on to college will find many obstacles to success. A large number of them will drop out during or after the first year. Ultimately, only fifteen of the original one hundred high school freshmen will become four-year degree graduates, meaning that 85 percent will not have reached that goal.[1]

These stats speak to a paradox many Latino immigrants feel: not being quite sure how to value the very thing they sacrificed so much for. Like all immigrant groups, Latinos who came to the U.S. did so seeking an opportunity to make better lives for themselves and their children. Many of these immigrants arrive without even a high school education and thus face limited employment opportunities. As strong believers in the American Dream, they seek the recipe for the "secret sauce" to achieve it. Hard work, rewarded more in the U.S. than it had been in their home countries, is a plus in their lives that they grasp tenaciously. However, regarding a higher education as important proves more elusive, given the relentless demands of a hand-to-mouth existence.

Most new arrivals and first-generation Latinos are often satisfied and parentally proud with their offspring if they graduate from high school, something they themselves may have been unable to do. They believe that with a high school diploma in hand, their sons and daughters will be able to find good jobs. Given the economic struggles faced by many of these families, their children need to go to work as soon as possible; indeed, it is likely crucial that they contribute to the family's survival. Going to college can be dismissed as a waste of time and money, possibly even considered a luxury.

The avenues for advancing into the middle class have become more limited. The decline of manufacturing in the U.S. means fewer middle-class jobs are available to those with limited education. Often the only path left for advancing into the middle class is a college diploma. To achieve success and a high-level career position in corporate America, it's the only way.

Cari Dominguez, the former executive with Bank of America, commented on the need to combine the values of hard work and a good education:

> My parents never begrudged their circumstances, because they just felt that it was well worth a sacrifice on their part for us to live in freedom and to get a good education. So what they said to us was, "You have to work hard, you have to get a good education, and you have to pay it forward whenever you have the opportunity. Make sure that you help those who are coming behind you, because this is a nation of immigrants. Everyone starts from the bottom and moves ahead with hard work and a good education.

Hard work will not be enough to advance Latinos in meaningful numbers into executive and senior management ranks. The Latino Executive Manifesto proclaims we must tackle this challenge with urgency and effective strategies that address the root causes of low Latino participation rates in college enrollment and graduation.

Latino Educational Achievement Trends

In its 25th anniversary report in 2011, the Hispanic Association of Colleges and Universities (HACU) noted, "Hispanic high school graduation rates and readiness for college are much lower for Latinos than their peers. In addition to (and in part because of) socioeconomic realities such as low income and low parental educational attainment, Hispanics are far more likely to attend under-resourced PK–12 schools." The report continues: "More limited school finances lead to inadequate and lower quality educational services. These socioeconomic and school resource and quality factors explain much of the research findings on dropouts and high school graduation."[2]

There are positive trends as well. Even though Hispanics trail other ethnic groups in earning bachelor's degrees (Figure 2), there is steady improvement as their high school dropout rate has fallen dramatically and college enrollment increased. The Pew Research Center reports that while in 2000, 32 percent of Latinos did not complete high school, by 2014 that rate had fallen 20 points to just 12 percent. That same year, 35 percent of those aged eighteen to twenty-four were enrolled in either a two- or four-year college, up

FIGURE 2

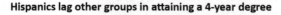

Hispanics lag other groups in attaining a 4-year degree

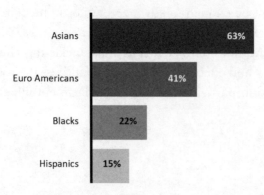

from 22 percent in 1993, a 13 percent increase. The number of European-American college students in that age group rose just 5 percentage points, to 42 percent; Black enrollment increased to 33 percent, rising 8 points in the same time frame.

Even with this increase in enrollment, just 15 percent of Hispanics have a bachelor's degree or higher, compared to 41 percent for European Americans, 22 percent for Blacks, and 63 percent for Asians. This is partly because they are less likely to attend a four-year college, choosing instead to enroll in two-year programs at community colleges (the highest share of any ethnicity), and are more likely to live at home while working and attending school part-time. (One bright side to this is that Latino households have significantly lower amounts of student debt.)

Because they are affordable, local, and positioned to serve a first-generation college student's needs, two-year community colleges—many of which have been designated as Hispanic-serving institutions (HSIs)—provide an opportunity for many Latino students who couldn't otherwise afford a four-year program.

HSIs were the result of legislation that emerged in 1992 when the HACU urged Congress to begin targeting campuses with high Hispanic enrollment for federal appropriations. Two- and four-year institutions must have a Hispanic enrollment total of more than 25 percent and be designated as an HSI to receive an increase of funds. Currently HSIs in the U.S. represent less than 10 percent of all higher education institutions nationwide, but together they enroll more than two-thirds of all Hispanic college students. Most HSIs are found in areas with increasing Hispanic populations including Miami, Detroit, Philadelphia, Chicago, Los Angeles, and San Antonio.

However, the welcome increased enrollment of Latinos in community colleges, HSIs, and other four-year schools is eroded by their higher dropout rate compared to European Americans. This must then be the next area of focus: to increase the Latino college graduate pipeline.

Why do Latinos falter? Put simply, they're often unprepared for college, since they can't rely on the shared experience of their parents having some college education to thus guide them. It's not that the families aren't willing to help them; rather, they just don't know how to do so.

The stakes are high to be able to enter college—and to remain there. Latinos often feel a sense of alienation and sometimes face animosity or unconscious biases. Many of the issues discussed in the earlier chapters about corporate America also relate to education. Lisa Garcia Quiroz, former senior vice president for Time Warner, reflects:

> I know plenty of people who went to Harvard, colleagues of mine, Latino students who entered the same time I did but who were back home by year's end because the environment was so alien and so White. The university wasn't great about supporting those students.

While the challenges are considerable after Latinos enter college, many headwinds prevent their even enrolling in the first place. Let's look at those issues.

THE LEGACY OF HIGH INTEREST RATES

Many Latino immigrants came from countries with very high rates of interest, sometimes more than 50 percent, which discourages going into debt. As a result, Latinos are uncomfortable with the idea of taking out loans for college. This leads to students paying cash for a semester and then taking time off when they can't afford the next tuition payment. They hope to be able to work to save enough to return to school. This pattern becomes a slippery slope: when they start taking semesters off, they extend the time it takes to get a degree, resulting in more of a challenge.

PEER PRESSURE

Latino kids' friends who are not college-bound often accuse someone who wants higher education of being "uppity" or "trying to be White" rather than understanding that they're simply trying to increase their chances for career success and financial security. Grace Lieblein, former vice president for General Motors, states:

> The gift that my mom gave me was a belief that I could do anything. I grew up thinking I can be anything I want to be. When we were seniors in high school, I told my friends I wanted to be an engineer. They were horrified: "You're going to be what? Is that on a train?" "No," I replied. My friends clearly did not understand me, but I had no fear of going into a nontraditional field at all.

LARGE FAMILIES

When younger children in large families who are living hand-to-mouth need basic necessities such as shoes or clothes, parents often discourage college attendance for the older children as an unaffordable luxury. As soon as children graduate from high school, they are expected to begin working full-time to bring in additional income. In these households, college tuition is seen not as an investment with future returns, but rather as an immediate cost that should be avoided.

HIGH RATES OF TEENAGE PREGNANCY

Although the rates of teenage pregnancy for Hispanics have fallen dramatically since 1990, one in three Latinas under age twenty becomes pregnant, which is one and a half times higher than the national average. Obviously, having the responsibility of raising a child lowers the likelihood of women attaining college degrees.

FAMILY TIES

Sometimes the strong emphasis on family prevents bright Latino students from going to the best schools because their families want them to remain close. This factor limits the number of colleges and universities some students even consider. And young Latinas face more pressure to remain close to family than do many European Americans.

Former ConAgra Consumer Foods President Lou Nieto recalls how this scenario played out in his family. Although he stayed close to home precisely because of the family pull, he was fortunate that the college close to home was a first-rate one. He recalls:

> I applied to a bunch of Ivy League schools and some in the Chicago area. My dream was to go East. I was accepted at Harvard College and thrilled about my fulfilled dreams. In late April, before I had to accept the East Coast school offer, my mother pulled me aside and asked if I would stay home in Chicago and not go away. I said yes, of course. I don't regret not going East because I certainly got a strong education at the University of Chicago.

CURRENT POLITICAL AND BUDGETARY CLIMATE

As if the headwinds facing Latino students were not enough, the current political landscape—driven by certain legislatures and governors who are not diversity-friendly—does not bode well for increasing educational opportunities for Latinos and other people of color.

Many states are cutting back dramatically on their support for public colleges and universities, at a time when the cost of higher education is growing at an almost exponential rate.

Illinois is a striking example. In 2017, Governor Bruce Rauner and the state legislature were at a budgetary standoff, so the state had no budget for three years. This resulted in draconian cuts at all state-supported institutions, including Northeastern Illinois University (NEIU) in Chicago, which serves a large number of first-generation and minority students, including many Latinos. In May 2017, NEIU was forced to eliminate about 180 full-time jobs.

The cuts included 130 civil service and fifty administrative and professional employees—a quarter of the staffing in both categories. These cuts are particularly harmful to Latino students. "They're your resources, your advisers, your mentors," Ashlei Ross, a NEIU senior and president of the student government association, told the *Chicago Tribune*. "They're the staff that are the ones who are really holding your hand. To lose that is a dramatic thing, especially for first-generation students because they don't have that resource at home. They can't ask their parents."[3]

Attitudes About Education

In spite of these headwinds, the growing push for education among Latinos feeds a telling contrast between Latino and European-American families. Often in middle-class Anglo communities higher education is seen as a given, almost part of the air their children breathe. The assumption is that their offspring will further their education, and when they don't choose to do so, those children are breaking the norm. In contrast, if young Latinos from low-income families do go to college, *that* is breaking the norm.

It is anecdotally shared among many Latinos that when you ask both Latino and Anglo parents if they're involved in their children's education, they'll each say yes. For the Anglo parents, that answer will likely mean they join the PTA and go to parent-teacher conferences. When the Hispanic parents say they're involved, it means their son or daughter has clean clothes and pencils. Although the Hispanic parents push their children to get good grades and better themselves, it's a different dynamic. They don't know the pathways: applying to schools, taking college tours, or discovering how to pay for an education.

Pew Hispanic Research reveals that the importance Latino families place on attaining a college education has markedly increased over the past few years. Eighty-eight percent of Latino families agree that a college degree is necessary to get ahead, versus only 74 percent of European Americans.[4] This shift in attitude is a driving factor in the growing numbers of Latinos enrolled in college. Luis Ubiñas, corporate board member for Electronic Arts, points out:

> Education is an anchor value of Latinos. We as a community take any scrap of opportunity for education. You see it in factory workers who try to send their kids to a better school in a better neighborhood. The mothers take extra jobs to pay for tutoring. Children are being raised with the idea that their education and subsequent opportunities are their responsibility. From both personal observation and my knowledge of higher education, I feel that the Latino community is desperate to get the educational advancement that is required.

These improvements in higher education have been fueled partly by Latino parents who figured out this key ingredient in the secret sauce of the American Dream, even if great sacrifice is required. Lou Nieto recalls those sacrifices made by his parents:

> I attended a small parochial school in our almost exclusively Latino community and the Franciscan sisters told my parents that St. Ignatius Prep (a Jesuit school) was the best school in the city. They added, "Your son should go there because he's a really good student." My parents sent me there, thus changing my life. My dad was a Teamster, so we were very blue collar. We weren't poor (I wouldn't try to pretend to be that) but we didn't think of ourselves as middle class either. My dad took a second job and my mom, a part-time job to be able to send my brother and me to Ignatius Prep. There was no financial aid back then. So just paying the high school tuition was a big sacrifice for my parents. They were big believers in education, and it paid off because it got us into good colleges.

In addition to parents who understand the role of education in creating more opportunities, other socioeconomic factors have contributed to the slow but steady increase of Latinos attending college. The onset of the 2008 recession led to a rise in unemployment for Latino youth, and ironically this increased their long-term economic prospects, since many chose to attend college in light of there not being any jobs.

Darren Rebelez, CEO of Casey's General Stores, told us:

> My dad had not gone to college; no one in his family did, yet he demanded that I get an education. He didn't know how we were going to pay for it, and he didn't know what I needed to do to get in, but he just expected it, and I needed to figure that out.

Grace Lieblein, who grew up middle class and had parents who attended college, did not necessarily face the same challenges that other Latinos who are from lower-income families face:

> My father was a huge proponent of education. His brothers and sisters were highly educated and had left Cuba, after Castro had taken over, with basically the clothes on their back. They were able to make good lives in other countries. Therefore he always said, "Material things can be taken away, but your education can never be taken away." If I was going to college was never in question. The assumption was always yes.

The Many Roads to the College Experience

The successful executives we interviewed had a wide range of educational experiences, depending on their family and community backgrounds.

Some grew up in Latin America in affluent families and came to the U.S. later in life, while others came from barrios in El Paso or Los Angeles. A few were the only Hispanics in their neighborhoods, while others came of age in communities of mixed ethnicities. There were those who attended prestigious colleges such as Stanford or Harvard, and others who began their education at local community colleges. Some faced discrimination and isolation because of their Latino backgrounds, but for others it didn't seem to matter. Cubans in Florida, Mexicans in Texas or California, Venezuelans in Illinois—all had interesting stories to tell about their experiences from grade school through college. All credited their educations as helping them to learn skills for their career path, and also in socializing with other ethnic groups, which enabled them to participate more fully in a broader society. Following are some of their stories.

DIFFERENT SCHOOL EXPERIENCES

Gilbert Casellas, former chairman of the U.S. Equal Employment Opportunity Commission, shares:

> I went to an all-black parochial school for the first six years. It was the same school my parents went to. The school had been founded in 1894 by Sisters of the Holy Name. When they established the school, the surrounding neighbors—who were all White— burnt it to the ground and posted a handwritten note on a tree nearby saying, "You educate these colored kids, they're not going to want to work."

Victor Arias, a managing director for Diversified Search, talked about attending Cathedral High School in El Paso:

> I remember there being more Mexican Americans than there were non-Mexican Americans. There was also a good number of Mexicanos from Ciudad Juarez, making the school population an interesting sort of mix. Even though I wasn't aware of it, those who actually lived in Ciudad Juarez were very different. I started realizing the differences between those who were just purely strong Mexican citizens versus the Mexican Americans, versus the gringos. Still, everybody really excelled.

Intel Chief People Officer Sandra Rivera, discussing her parents' emphasis on education, told us:

> The importance of education—and more than that, the culture and the love of learning—was instilled in us. From a very early age we were taught that an education, a good education, was the path that would really open up all these opportunities in life.

Former McDonald's Executive Vice President José Armario recounts how his time in a military school helped him succeed:

> Through grade school and middle school, I first attended the public school system and then a private military school, Miami Aerospace Academy. That experience, while it was very tough, created a lot of good habits for me in terms of study, homework, testing—attaining success early in life by being very disciplined.

José graduated from Miami Dade Community College with an associate's degree in business administration. He then began attending a local college in pursuit of his bachelor's degree, but left the program because he just didn't find it inspiring. He rose rapidly through the corporate hierarchy at Burger King and was busy launching a successful career. College really didn't matter at that point. Ultimately, when he was in his forties, José decided that he wanted to finish his education and acquired a master's degree. Speaking of his experience at the University of Miami, he told us:

> They had an advertisement for pursuing a master's degree that didn't require a four-year degree. When I met with the admissions officers, they said, "Since you don't have the four-year degree, but have extensive experience, we just need you to take the graduate admissions test. If you do well on the test, we always admit one student who doesn't have a bachelor's degree." I was that student! Fifteen months later I had a master of science in management.

Lou Miramontes, a retired KPMG partner, lived at home while attending California State University, East Bay. He recounts his experience:

I think about my parents' income and how they really didn't have the college funds for us, although college wasn't that expensive back then. Given their income level and our situation, sending me to college was still going to be an effort, so I lived at home. I remember telling my dad that everybody else had a bunch of roommates and were living in dorms. He said, "You did pretty well at home in high school, *amigo*." I had no problem understanding that because I was close to Mom, Dad, and my brothers. Since I didn't want to incur any costs for them, I lived at home and kept working hard at college.

LUCKY BREAKS AND MENTORS

Many of these successful executives had a lucky break that changed the course of their educational careers. Darren Rebelez remembers attending a college fair with his father after having attended his less-than-challenging high school in Southern California:

I was just grabbing the normal California college giveaways from the U.C. system, San Diego State, and others. West Point happened to have a booth there. My dad asked, "Why don't you go talk to those guys?" I countered, "How am I going to get in there, Dad? You're not a congressman or a general." He said, "Shut up and get an application." I did, I applied, and I was accepted.

Some executives had caring mentors who helped them greatly in getting accepted by top-notch schools. For Gilbert Casellas, that guidance came from a priest and a doctor who helped him get into Yale. He recalls:

> In my senior year in high school, as I'm applying for colleges, one of the priests came to me saying he had been at a dinner party where the doctor who was the host was a graduate of Yale and Harvard and was really interested in recruiting minority students. This priest said, "Y'know, I told him about you, and I thought you should talk to him and consider applying to Yale and Harvard. I'm going to put you in touch with him and he's going to contact you."

> I added Yale to my application list. I received a thick envelope from them on April 4, 1970—you don't forget certain dates. I was stunned and will remember forever my dad's words when he read the letter: "Hell of an opportunity!" That's all he said, and that did it for me. I accepted.

Education as the Great Equalizer

It's clear that a college education expands horizons for first-generation students by exposing them to new understandings of the broader world. They learn middle-class conventions and new values of speaking, dressing, critical thinking, problem-solving, and more. These lessons don't come from going to class, but instead are embedded in the way the students absorb the college life. No matter how smart you are, if you don't go to college, you will very likely miss out on so much that underlies the middle-class corporate culture.

Most importantly, during college, students begin to build and take advantage of personal networks, which leads to contacts who can later open doors in the business world. Latino organizations such as Society of Hispanic Professional Engineers (SHPE) and ALPFA have college chapters that offer opportunities for Hispanic students to join together and expand their networks. University alumni associations also provide another way to make important connections.

These expanded horizons create a ripple effect that goes beyond the individual students, spreading through their immediate and extended families, and into the community at large. Graduates who earn degrees and begin working in corporations enlarge their social circle and may travel the U.S. and even other countries. They share those experiences with family and friends, giving others a glimpse of more possibilities for themselves. Rather than being viewed as "uppity," these people become role models for others in their community who begin to seek similar opportunities. This ripple effect encourages others to follow a similar path.

Here's Victor Arias, speaking of his experience at Stanford University:

> I learned how to bob and weave because of the challenges I faced, and that's when I felt, *S***, you know, I belong here. Nobody's going to tell me I don't belong.* I gained incredible confidence about what I could accomplish. I learned that having attended Stanford opened a lot of doors, so I just feel a tremendous amount of gratitude toward Stanford. I didn't have a lot of money so I decided to give them a lot of my time when I got out of school, and I did so. Stanford's a very special place, and I reiterate that it opened many doors for me.

Luis Ubiñas, who grew up in a poor neighborhood in the South Bronx with a father who had substance abuse issues, describes how he was able to rise above his home circumstances:

> I had the good fortune of having, through finan-
> cial aid, a scholarship to go to private schools
> in Manhattan. After that I ended up at Harvard
> College, where I graduated magna cum laude and
> got accepted to Harvard Business School.

Luis recalls being accepted by the other students in the tony private schools, occasionally spending nights at their homes—although it was out of the question for them to come to his:

> Going into those friends' homes was like going on
> a vacation, perhaps a safari. You may feel welcome,
> but you don't necessarily feel comfortable. When
> you are from the projects—buildings burning on
> the horizon and criminals literally blocking your
> path from your front door to the subway—arriving
> at a heated, private school on the Upper East Side
> where there was a fantastic education awaiting me
> was nothing short of a blessing.

Unintended Consequence: Education as an Unequalizer

There is also a potential pitfall to Latinos attaining a college degree: education as an unequalizer. This situation occurs when the first-generation college graduate comes away with a sense of superiority to their less-educated family members and friends. It may lead to alienation, distrust, embarrassment, and other destructive emotions. This works both ways, as the young man or woman with the college degree may see their family or friends as uninformed, naïve, unmotivated, or dull, while the other side sees the graduate as pretentious, dismissive, and even in denial of their Latino heritage—trying to be European American.

Recognizing this unconscious bias against your own culture requires courage and self-awareness, and then humility to overcome it. When graduates don't address their attitudes, this unequalizing factor causes some to become Invisible Latinos.

Ultimately, education has created both the foundation and the propulsion to success for the Latino executives we interviewed.

Completing college requires supportive parents or, if parents weren't supportive, self-agency, mentors and sponsors, scholarships, plain luck, and blessings. Individuals must have the tenacity to face the myriad headwinds, as Lisa Garcia Quiroz explains:

> I was used to being the only one [Latina] and saw persevering as a challenge. I had a sense of being given an incredible opportunity that I couldn't fail. To me, it wasn't even an option to go back. Go back to what?

Advancing their education is becoming easier for Latinos. Graduation rates are improving for both high school and college. HSIs are helping two-thirds of Latino college students. Other Latino organizations providing help are college alumni associations. For example, the Latino Alumni Association at USC has given over $15 million in scholarships to Latino students since 1973, while at Cornell University the Latino Alumni Association focuses on the recruitment and retention of Latino students.

A recurring theme of the executives we've profiled is their commitment to pay it forward. Nowhere is this more important than in working to improve the prospects of college-bound Latinos.

As demographic trends continue to indicate, the workforce of the future will have an increasingly Latino identity. Challenges that impact Latino student success are an issue not only for Latinos but also for the entire U.S. As Latino education attainment rises, so does economic opportunity for the entire country.

A BOLD WAY TO BUILD THE DIVERSE TALENT PIPELINE

In its May-June 2017 issue, *Harvard Business Review*[5] details a successful program in Boston to integrate all the efforts of various nonprofit organizations focused toward the goal of Latinos and other minorities successfully completing college and securing a good job. It profiles State Street Capital CEO Scott Nobles. When Nobles was appointed to a Massachusetts public/private workforce development program, he saw a lack of coordination among agencies.

Given the challenges of urban education, he realized that effective intervention must go beyond what happens in classrooms. He said, "Getting students through school, into college, and then into good jobs requires managing a series of hand-offs and transitions. For example, some nonprofits do a great job of coaching high school students to improve their study skills or to perform better on college admissions exams. But rarely do those same organizations help the students with the college search and application process, which is the logical next step. Other organizations do that, but many kids can't navigate between the two. Then, when students get into college, they need mentoring and coaching to help them stay enrolled and succeed, which requires a different kind of support. After that they need help getting ready for a job and finding one. It's similar to a hospital experience: The patient may be treated by several specialists, and they have to communicate well with one another to achieve overall success."

In 2015 the State Street Foundation set up a program called Boston WINs (Workforce Investment Network). They staged a *Shark Tank*–like competition for local nonprofits, committing to an investment of $20 million over the next four years and to hiring one thousand of the program's graduates. The goal was a seamless program that combined all the necessary expertise to support youths from high school through college and into the workplace. They chose a handful of nonprofits who had proven records, gave them funding to scale up, and taught them to coordinate their efforts so they were no longer working in isolation.

After seeing a successful outcome over two years, Nobles concludes, "We're nearly halfway through our four-year commitment to Boston WINs, and we've already hired two hundred grads. We're already thinking about how to scale the program beyond Boston, to other parts of the country and the world."

CHAPTER 6

How to Be: Three Key Traits of Transformational Leaders

El que sigue la consigue.

Who perseveres, achieves.

—Anonymous

Battle hardened by facing the outer forces of corporate culture biases and cultural identity crises, Latino executives have also developed and honed particular leadership competencies, traits, and philosophies, enabling their success as transformative Latino leaders.

One key objective in our research was to discover these secrets to their success. So far in this journey we have extensively explored the foundational requirement of being *auténtico*, which the Latino Executive Manifesto declares must entail both defining and embracing our Latino cultural identity.

On top of the foundation of cultural authenticity, what did the executives we interviewed learn and put into play to become transformational leaders? Six key elements surfaced—three traits and three competencies:

TRAITS
- Embracing ambition as an honorable intent
- Risk-taking as a catalyst for growth and getting noticed
- Deeply valuing relationships

COMPETENCIES
- Political savvy about corporate culture
- Establishing and shaping one's own leadership style
- Giving back to the community

We elaborate on the three traits in this chapter and on the three competencies in the next.

Embrace Ambition as Honorable

The executives' response to the inherent fatalism of Latino culture discussed in chapter 4 is recognizing that corporate America is not waiting for Latinos to wake up and take their seat at the executive table. Latinos must pursue these positions with vigor and ambition. It is thus no surprise that each of our Latino executives demonstrated elevated ambition and a deep desire to be successful in all aspects of life. They wanted to feel success and to be seen as successful, often to be seen as role models for other Latinos, or to be a tribute to their families for the many sacrifices made on their behalf.

It's easy to confuse ambition with aspiration, but they are not the same. Mere aspiration tends to focus on a particular goal; ambition is more of a trait or disposition, and as such is persistent and pervasive. The word "ambition" comes from the Latin word *ambitio* (a striving for honor, recognition, and preferment). To be ambitious is to achieve—not just for the sake of achievement itself but also for distinguishing ourselves from others.

Ambition is also different from hope. Hope is the desire for something to happen, and anticipation of its happening. In contrast, ambition is the desire for achievement and distinction *combined* with the willingness to strive for—as well as take—the necessary steps for success. Ambition is more self-propelled than hope.

Let's look at some of the characteristics of ambition.

ACHIEVING SUCCESS REQUIRES A DEEP-SEATED COMMITMENT

The Latino executives we interviewed proved to have talent and ability, but most important, they also had *ganas*, that hard-to-translate Latino cultural term that alludes to pursuing endeavors with total heart, body, mind, and soul. Their ambition drove them to dedicate their lives to long hours and hard work, the perfection of a craft, and a willingness to sacrifice for the sake of reaching the level they wished to attain.

It's clear that most come from family environments full of ambition and determination, the foundation for their own personal ambition. Many described parents whose attitudes led them to overcome obstacles and to triumph against significant odds. Immediate and extended family demonstrated the dream and the drive that proved having ambition was more important than having natural ability or access to resources.

For example, Gilbert Casellas's father was a high school dropout, yet he always encouraged his son to do well in school—even when Gilbert was required to attend segregated schools in Tampa. Yvonne Garcia's father did not go to school past the seventh grade, yet he recognized that education was the key to freedom and economic mobility. Lou Miramontes remembers his dad having to go to work at four in the morning as a migrant worker, always working extra hours so he could support the family. Getting a good education and going to a Catholic school was so important to Victor Arias's family; his dad worked two jobs so they could afford school tuition.

When Lou Nieto's school was forced to desegregate after the *Brown v. Board of Education* ruling, his mom, a civil rights activist, fought the school administration to make sure Lou was enrolled in the best classes at his school. She had big ambitions for him, hoping that he would someday become a U.S. senator. Lou's own goal was to become the CEO of a Fortune 500 company.

Charlie Garcia's ambition to be in public service was influenced by his father, who served the government of Panama in various roles throughout his career. With that model of public service, Charlie studied at the Air Force Academy and began a military career. His mom was a public school teacher for twenty-two years, sparking Charlie's passion for education—which eventually led him to serve a White House Fellowship for Bill Bennett (Secretary of Education) and five years on the State Board of Education in Florida.

Monica Lozano's grandfather crossed the border into the U.S. from Mexico. He very much believed in the power of the press and was ambitious enough to eventually start two newspapers, one in San Antonio and one in Los Angeles. Luis Ubiñas's grandmother came from Puerto Rico with eight children, eventually settling on the Lower East Side of New York City. His mother, the eldest of those children, had to leave school early to work helping support the family. Luis earned scholarships to attend private schools, often having to avoid gangs and violence on his way to class. He would later attend both Harvard College and Harvard Business School.

Several of our executives come from families courageous and ambitious enough to flee Cuba and the Castro regime. Grace Lieblein's father left Cuba in 1951, before Castro seized control. He came to the U.S. to attend college but ended up enlisting in the Army and serving in the Korean War.

José Armario's father was an outspoken critic of the Communist regime and had to flee Cuba in fear for his life. José and his family soon followed.

Cari Dominguez's family reached the U.S. in a different order than José's; her father was under house surveillance when she left Cuba at age twelve with her mom and two sisters. Her dad joined the family in Maryland six years later. Myrna Soto's father was a political prisoner for a time before leaving Cuba to go into exile. Even though Myrna's mother did not graduate from high school, her parents always expected her to do well in school.

Ambition provided the stimulus for State Street's Yvonne Garcia to seek out leadership roles to be in a stronger position to drive change:

> I've always felt comfortable in a leadership role. I've never really liked being second place, I never really enjoyed being vice-chair, and I don't enjoy being a vice-president. I've always enjoyed leading something because I have this combination of the ability to be strategic. But I also have a strong bias toward execution. I feel that when you are in charge of leading something, you're able to take action much quicker, influence people much faster, and drive change faster because you're able to make decisions.

What all these stories demonstrate is that transformational Latino leaders found motivation in the struggles and sacrifices their families faced. They felt an obligation to be ambitious and to give extra effort. The opportunities afforded to them were fought for and won by past family members. However, these opportunities were given to them with an implicit contract—that they make the most of them. Anything less than a high level of success and ambition would dishonor the efforts demonstrated by their families.

FORGET THE NAYSAYERS

While immediate family may have been mostly supportive of their early ambitions, what further distinguishes these executives was their ability to overcome naysayers who deemed their ambitions a negative trait. ¿Qué te crees? is a Hispanic sentiment that loosely translated means "Who do you think you are?" It was an expression they often heard from classmates, neighbors, and eventually other Latino professionals who considered them cocky for having such ambition. Lou Miramontes recalls some of his Hispanic friends making fun of him for trying so hard in his classes and hanging out with the smart Anglo students. They mocked him by asking, "Are you trying to be White?" Lou's response was, "No, I'm trying to be successful."

The secret to becoming a transformational leader is not merely having ambition, but keeping a distance from those who feel that big ambition is something to be ashamed of. Latinos must learn that outside of this small group of detractors—who are rarely good role models anyway—denying your ambition does not make you seem humble; rather, it makes you seem insecure. Denying your ambition does not make you seem unpretentious; it makes you appear unfocused. It does not make you look modest; it makes you look like you aren't in control of your life.

What distinguished our Latino executives was not a denial of the strain of fatalism that courses through Latino culture, but rather a higher sense of self-efficacy. *They held a strong belief that their ambitious actions could produce the outcomes they desired.* This belief gave them the added motivation to embark on their pursuits and persevere in the face of adversity. Heavy ambition should not be confused with greed or hubris; it should be seen as a desire to escape mediocrity.

Another distinguishing strategy for the Latino executives was making sure they succeeded *because* of the naysayers. They saw their detractors as doubtful, critical, and envious. They used the negative noise to fuel their ambition and prove the naysayers wrong via an "I'll show them" mentality. For example, on his acceptance into Yale University, Gilbert Casellas recalls his high school guidance counselor telling him that Yale was a hotbed for radicalism and that "Yale is going to screw you royally." Gilbert's response: "Talk about a motivator. I'm going to show you. I never saw him again, but in terms of the drive, those are the kind of remarks that cut deep."

Many of our Latino executives were at one time considered underdogs, but through their ambition they were able to demonstrate to others that they were being underestimated. Juan Galarraga recalls being named a group director at Target, one of the youngest at the time. He started to hear people questioning his promotion, deeming it the result of minority hiring policies rather than his capability. Instead of getting angry or defensive, he used the comments to further drive his performance and to show others that he had indeed earned—and deserved—the promotion.

Lou Nieto's ambition was fueled in part by a desire to quiet his critics:

> I've always had this compulsion to excel and do well, because I've run into so many people in my life who try to diminish what you accomplish by saying, "You probably got into Harvard

because you're Latino" or "You probably got into University of Chicago because you're Latino." I always feel it's not good enough to be just as good as the people around me, because somebody can try to diminish it. So I've always strived to be better than everybody around me.

GOOD ENOUGH IS NOT ENOUGH

Our transformational leaders described how they mentor younger Latinos to also be ambitious. Myrna Soto tells her mentees to never be satisfied with good enough, and to always strive for more. Similarly, José Armario advises young Latinos to never back down, and to develop a *fire in the belly* for professional growth. He tells them about one of his secrets to success:

> Number one was I never backed down from taking on a more difficult job or challenging project, because I wanted to show my skills and to learn from the work accomplished. I never backed away, even though it meant more work. I always found that there was more to gain than to lose. My advice to young Latinos: "Take on more and challenge yourself."

Likewise, Monica Lozano shares this with Latino millennials:

> I'm a firm believer in raising your hand and your voice. It's important for others to know that you consider yourself prepared to take the next step. Leaders don't lean back, they lean in, and they stand up in order to be recognized for their work, their talent, and their contributions. It's important to demonstrate a desire to stretch, to expand networks, to learn new things, and to be exposed to new situations.

The lesson for the next generation of Latino leaders is to not be afraid to think big, and to express your expectation of achieving great things. When Latinos hedge their ambitions and dreams because they want to be "realistic," their success is diminished by that hedging. Without a high sense of ambition, Latino professionals will achieve only modest growth. Without high ambition, people may eventually realize that their static career is self-imposed. They have taken only small steps up the career ladder because they sought nothing more. If becoming a CEO or C-suite executive seems like an alien idea, it may be that they haven't been sufficiently convinced to believe it's possible.

These transformational Latinos did not settle for what they *could have*; rather, they pursued what they *wanted*. Their ambition helped them have a career based on the premise of pursuit; they took the offensive. They discovered that a conservative approach was not for them. In their upward mobility, they further validated that their ambition was crucial. Along the way they realized that the struggle gave them strength, much like the tempering of steel.

In the quest to fill the pipeline of future Latino leaders, we must acknowledge that ambition is a good thing and must be encouraged.

Risk-Taking as a Catalyst for Growth and Getting Noticed

As we've described in earlier chapters, Latinos should not shoulder an additional burden of proof in workplace performance that is not expected of non-Latinos. Latinos often work under a burden of flawed assumptions and negative stereotypes. They often live with the reality of facing harsher consequences for even small missteps. For these reasons, Latinos may feel exposed, vulnerable, and insecure throughout their careers. They worry that any mistake might make them look bad, so they can be prone to freeze up or take the safe route.

And yet, the Latino executives we interviewed taught us that without having the courage to take career chances, Latino professionals cannot expect to, as Price Cobbs famously said, "crack the corporate code." It is clear from their stories that Latino professionals must give themselves permission to be pioneers and to explore career opportunities that may not have guarantees. They must be open to following a path without a clear roadmap. To be a transformative Latino leader requires being comfortable taking risks.

Next, we look at some of their tips for taking those risks.

TAKING RISKS MEANS ABANDONING EXCUSES FOR NOT TAKING ON OPPORTUNITIES THAT STRETCH US

Avoiding risks is impossible in a career; something is always at stake, so it's a matter of deciding which risks to take. Transformational leaders do view risk-taking not as a gamble, but rather as making a move on an opportunity they may have ignored in the past. We've learned from these executives that effective risk-taking means being able to abandon excuses and realize that often all that is really standing in the way of upward career mobility is oneself.

For example, we noticed that transformational leaders have a unique perspective on *developmental job assignments*—those ad hoc projects that pop up out of organizational necessity. These may not necessarily be part of a job description, but they require a volunteer to complete the project. Taking on such assignments means the aspiring Latinos are seen as more valuable to the organization; it's an opportunity to visibly test themselves and be tested. These assignments allow volunteers to demonstrate their capabilities as decision-makers, giving them the chance to make their mark and be noticed.

Darren Rebelez of Casey's General Stores took unconventional risks that accelerated his advancement. After successfully working in operations in the food service and restaurant industry, he took a developmental assignment in marketing and category management—areas he knew very little about. This broadened his skillset tremendously, giving him the opportunity to work with franchise owners. The franchise experience was instrumental in propelling him to the chief operating officer position at 7-Eleven, and ultimately to become the president of IHOP.

> You have to be willing to explore some possibilities, try some new things, and put yourself in a position to potentially fail if you expect to succeed down the road. Not everything's going to be easy for you, so at a certain point you have to decide, "I'm going to take a chance," whether that chance is going to a new company or even trying different jobs within a company.
>
> When I look at my career, I can't say that I had a linear career path. It was untraditional. I've seen so many times where people have had an opportunity to do something different that's a little bit out of their comfort zone, they say, "Yeah, that's not really the job I want; I want to do this other thing." I tell people, "That's OK, but you have to understand that when the decision-makers ask about who to put in the next advanced role, if you lack the experiences that the other candidates have, you're probably not going to get the job. You must

> recognize that if you're not willing to do some of those other jobs because you're afraid, that's your decision, but if you don't take that risk, you're not going to be as competitive for the roles that everybody's aspiring to."

Latino leaders must also recognize when career moves are too cautious. Beware of the trap when successive jobs do not move you beyond the zone of familiarity, security, and comfort. Cari Dominguez, the board director at ManpowerGroup, recalls early in her career being asked by one of her bosses to take a role that did not really stretch her skills or add new experiences in her preferred professional direction. She saw the potential risks this might pose for her future career aspirations. Feeling she wasn't growing enough, she decided to leave the corporate sector for a political appointment position at the U.S. Department of Labor.

At first, the move seemed counterintuitive—leaving the corporate world for a political role when most individuals in a political job are vying for a corporate position, which she already had. Political posts are full of uncertainties, reputational risks, and potential failure. However, she stacked those risks against the potential professional stagnation that she could have faced by accepting a role of limited growth and possibilities within the status quo. She saw that public policy-making offered her new opportunities to broaden her skills, gain new career credentials, and build new networks in a brand-new field, and, in the spirit of a transformational leader, she proceeded as if success was guaranteed. After successfully leading the department's Glass Ceiling Initiative, which was designed to remove artificial employment barriers affecting the advancement of women and minorities, Cari was appointed assistant secretary of labor by President George H. W. Bush. And having seen her work during his father's administration, President George W. Bush appointed Cari to serve as chair of the U.S. Equal Employment Opportunity Commission, one of his very first appointments. Both her private and public sector experiences ultimately provided the foundation she needed to become a corporate director. Clearly her risk-taking paid off.

A willingness to take risks does not mean that Latinos can be careless about their career path. Sloppy, halfhearted job moves will benefit a career very little. Successful Latino leaders view new jobs as a laboratory. They use each assignment to attempt new projects and to experience new environments. But more important, they realize that even if a particular position doesn't lead to advancement, each assignment contributes to their future path to success. Experience is the ultimate teacher, and both having great credentials as well as having broad experiences are keys to being noticed for promotion.

Accomplished Latino executives did not let the fear of failure consume them. They realized that doubt can do much damage in career moves. They did not give mental space to that doubt or fear of failure. They also recognized that waiting until they were absolutely ready was simply a stalling tactic. Even when not 100 percent ready, they took career risks and proceeded into new roles as if failure was inconceivable.

TAKING RISKS LEADS TO BEING NOTICED
Juan Galarraga's career may not have been possible without his taking some early risks. First, he came to the U.S. to go to college, even though he did not speak English. Later, he took another big risk: accepting an hourly wage job even though he had a college degree. He took a job unloading trucks at Target, beginning at 2 a.m. each day.

Juan continued to take risks with assignments throughout his career, which resulted in a meteoric rise through the ranks at Target. For example, after being an assistant manager for only a year, he was asked to fill in as a store manager for ninety days while the current manager was on leave. He realized that being asked to take this assignment meant that he was on the radar of top Target leaders. He didn't hesitate, and took the job even though he was not sure he was quite ready. When the manager decided not to return from leave, Juan took over as the store manager, even though he was only twenty-four years old. He recalls:

> Running that store felt incredibly intimidating. At a very young age, I was responsible for a $30 million store with close to two hundred team members. All of my assistant managers were more experienced, potentially more qualified, older than me—and I had worked for several of them previously.

What we can learn from Juan's move into the store manager position is that taking risks isn't about *taking* a big chance, but rather *giving* oneself a big chance. Latinos can take heart in knowing they have been fielding similar challenges and over coming them for most of our lives.

Juan's next move involved turning around a store location that was considered to be underperforming. His willingness to take a gamble and move to a different city—even when he didn't always realize the full extent of an opportunity—enabled him to acquire additional skills and gain more confidence. He explains:

> After a year and a half of running a store, I get a phone call to move to Naples, Florida, to take over a high-volume, highly visible, broken store. It had years of struggling operationally, and low team

morale. The phone call I got at the time: "Hey, we have this great opportunity where you can end up getting promoted or fired." Those were the type of things I applied for. I jumped on it! I felt like it was a great opportunity because I knew how to run a store; now I have the ability to turn a store around.

One morning Juan gathered everyone he managed at that store and had them write out their complaints, frustrations, and disappointments on pieces of paper. He then had them light a bonfire he'd set up behind the store and toss their pieces of paper into the flames. He explains:

I called a mandatory all-team meeting with everyone at 6 a.m. Most team members did not know who I was at that time because the first few days I was there, I had been working overnight in the back room. But as they went to the back of the store, they saw this big bonfire. They looked at me with a look of "What's going on?" I asked everyone to write down a story of something that was going on at the store that they didn't like or that didn't make them feel good. Then everyone, one after the other, read what they had written. When we were done, I had them throw their pieces of paper in the bonfire and I said, "No more, it's a new day, a new life, let's have each other's back. Today, we start anew!" I had heard them, and they had heard each other. That day we began turning that store around to the point where it became one of the most successful ones in the region.

And so it was. From that point on, he kept taking leadership risks with that store and its team, and in a few months, Juan successfully turned the store around. Morale was up, as were sales and profitability.

Juan's performance, risk-taking, and confidence led to a rapid string of promotions. By age twenty-eight he was a group director running a $2 billion business unit with one hundred stores. His next move required him to relocate to Target's corporate head-quarters in Minneapolis. He continued to excel, soon earning the title of vice president of healthcare operations. Then came another call, asking him to take over a region. Not even thirty-five years old, he was now a leader of a $17 billion business with five hundred stores in seventeen states.

Juan's accelerated career trajectory did lead to some adversity and increased scrutiny by others who thought he was too young for some of his roles. He is currently the senior vice president of retail operations for Five Below, a position he credits in part to his willing-ness to take career risks. Other Latinos can learn from him that a willingness to take risks early and throughout a career not only pro-vides new skills, experiences, and increased visibility, but also helps build much-needed confidence to take on even greater challenges.

José Armario includes a willingness to relocate as a key part of accepting risk. He notes:

> I was one of the few people in my group who fol-lowed opportunity no matter where it went. I wasn't afraid to move, to take on the next job. A lot of my friends stayed and waited for the next job because they didn't want to relocate, and sometimes those next jobs never materialized.

George Herrera, the current board director at Wyndham Destinations, believes that it is always better to try and then fail than to play it safe. People learn from mistakes, which helps them grow. He credits this approach for his willingness to take over the family business at a young age and growing it into a much larger company. He took this same approach when he was asked to become the first non-Mexican American to lead the U.S. Hispanic Chamber of Commerce as CEO.

Gilbert Casellas recalls the risk he took in leaving a well-paying job at a prestigious law firm for a judicial clerkship. It was a calculated risk, but one that eventually opened many more doors for him. It also helped him become a partner at his original law firm when he returned from the clerkship—a faster route than if he had played it safe and not taken the clerkship position.

Deeply Valuing Relationships

Transformational Latino leaders must also know how to cultivate relationships, both inside and outside their organization. Those we interviewed shared numerous stories of how investing in and nurturing relationships helped them find people who would give them honest feedback, help them access critical information, and commit themselves to the interviewee's future success. In fact, cultivating relationships was so vital to all the executives interviewed that it is the topic in our research that generated the most content, by a wide margin.

Paul Raines, the former CEO of GameStop, sums up the importance of relationships—one of his personal keys to success:

> You have to build relationships. They are so important because they carry you along the rest of your career. Those relationships you're building right now with that mid-level manager, or your boss, or your colleagues— those people will continue to grow, and they will carry you with them. So build solid

relationships. Those can be Latino relationships, or they can be non-Latino relationships. They can be in professional societies or whatever relationships are available to you. Maximize them! Take advantage of them!

Investing in and nurturing relationships requires a variety of strategies. Let's explore what the executives had to share.

RELATIONSHIPS HELP OVERCOME ISOLATION OR FEELING LIKE AN OUTSIDER

Patricia Diaz Dennis, the former AT&T executive and now board director at Amalgamated Bank, recalls the important support her relationships provided when she was the first Latina at a major Los Angeles law firm:

> This is where it started becoming obvious to me that I was different. I joined the Mexican-American Bar Association because I needed support from people who were like me, who grew up in the way I did. It was such a wonderful camaraderie. I really needed networks of people with whom I didn't have to explain trivial things. I felt like it was home. We would be able to share about how hard law school was for most of us, how hard we had to work, how proud we made our parents, how we were still kind of isolated at our jobs, and how we needed to support each other.
>
> Exposing your vulnerability is really tough, especially when you're in your first job. You learn to call your buddies, somebody in another firm who's done something similar, and ask for advice. "How do I handle this without seeming stupid to the person

I'm working with?" There's that anxiety in all of us. I'm sure this was true for all young people just starting out in their jobs, but it was heightened by the fact that most of us were among the very few Latinos and Latinas in our law firms or among the very few in our companies. We needed a safe place where we could ask questions.

CAPITALIZE ON THE FACT THAT SENIOR EXECUTIVES ARE CONSTANTLY ON THE LOOKOUT FOR NEW TALENT

In organizational settings, you don't find sponsors; sponsors find you. Getting yourself on the radar of senior executives or potential sponsors requires a reputation for performance excellence. Charlie Garcia, the former CEO of Sterling Financial Group and CEO of Tendrel, has a story of how being noticed the first time generated a ripple effect. After excelling at the Air Force Academy and distinguishing himself as an intelligence officer in the military, Charlie was spotted by four-star General John Galvin. Charlie was soon traveling with Galvin to meet with other generals, dignitaries, and presidents of foreign countries, as well as conducting briefings for the Senate Armed Services Committee.

Based on the superior quality of his work for General Galvin, Charlie next caught the eye of Mort Zuckerman, owner of *U.S. News and World Report*. Zuckerman encouraged him to apply for the White House Fellows Program and wrote a letter of recommendation on his behalf. Soon Charlie was in the program, and his fellowship spanned parts of both the Reagan and George H. W. Bush administrations. During this time he established relationships with William Bennett, former secretary of education, and John Whitehead, deputy secretary of state and former chairman of Goldman Sachs, both of whom became lifelong career advisors.

BUILD RELATIONSHIPS OUTSIDE YOUR COMFORT ZONE— WHICH MEANS NOT JUST IN LATINO CIRCLES

While connecting with other Latinos has proven to be a successful way to leverage relationships, Latinos often make the mistake— particularly early in their careers—of cultivating relationships with only people who are similar to them or who are part of their peer group.

Transformational leaders look outside their immediate circle and develop relationships with people who are not like them: people who work at different companies, who have different skillsets, or who belong to different peer groups. George Herrera encourages young Latinos to build relationships outside their comfort zone:

> If you're looking to go up those rungs and enter the corporate boardroom, you're going to need to start socializing and gathering at events where those individuals are. Approximately 99.9 percent of those events are not exclusively Hispanic events. I know that in the Latino community we're very culturally attuned to each other because we love family and we want to be in a family. But if you're born and raised in Miami and that opportunity is in Boise, Idaho, you should choose to move. Then you should learn that you must get out of your comfort zone and network outside of groups that have Latino relevance.

> Developing relationships with non-Latinos doesn't mean that you give up your culture; it doesn't mean that you give up your pride. It means that you must learn that you need to circulate in the circles where your immediate boss and some of the potential board members may be socializing so they will begin to see you in their environment. I think that's

something we really don't do often enough or well enough. We're scared and beat up with trepidation.

Monica Lozano recounts how her intention to get more involved and build relationships with community leaders outside of her day-to-day circles resulted in a sponsorship relationship that helped her career tremendously:

> With regard to networking and relationship-building, I was doing a lot of work with local, small nonprofit organizations and was asked to join the board of the YMCA for Greater Los Angeles. I accepted because I thought it would a great place for me to stay connected to community organizations and community leaders. Little did I know that these board members were the civic and business leaders of L.A. Through that experience I met the president of a regional bank, and over time he asked me to join his board of directors, my first such position. I recognize him to this day as being the person who gave me a start on corporate boards.

Monica's ability to cultivate relationships has been a critical component in her career success, which includes serving as a board director for the Walt Disney Company, Bank of America, and Target Corporation, and as a member of the board of trustees for USC, as well as on President Obama's Council on Jobs and Competitiveness.

Cari Dominguez also advises young Latinos who are establishing relationships to seek common ground with allies beyond the boundaries of race, ethnicity, class, gender, or age:

> By extending yourself, you'll find meaningful relationships, and they will find you, often in surprising and unexpected places. It's great to be within your

network, but the people who will most likely sponsor you and will support you and serve as references are those who are, for the most part, outside of that network. The people that have supported me and facilitated opportunities for advancement have not come from the Latino community. For example, the deputy assistant secretary of labor was an American University graduate, so when he found out I was an AU graduate, he took an interest in my career. When I was at Bank of America, I found another connection. My boss came from IBM, and I happened to have had some good friends from IBM, so we bonded through common friends. That relationship showed me that to get ahead I had to break new ground and try not to stay exclusively in the Latino circle of influence and support.

For Latino professionals like Charlie Garcia who grew up in Latin America, building relationships outside the family may be a new phenomenon:

I would say that I wasn't good at networking and had to change by asking for help and developing relationships outside of the family. In Latin America, you asked your immediate family for help if you needed it; help was in the family unit. You didn't network and ask questions and favors from people outside of the family. So networking was something that I had to learn to do, and it wasn't easy.

TRUST IS THE FOUNDATION OF RELATIONSHIPS

Trust was cultivated by our transformational leaders by showing that they cared for others, were able to guard confidences, could keep promises, and had the best interest of others in mind. Darren Rebelez states:

> I've always strived to build good relationships and trust with people. That doesn't always mean we're buddies, but you must establish trust with people.

George Herrera recalls a time when, as CEO of the Hispanic Chamber of Commerce, he was challenging a corporation's unfair practices in dealing with the Hispanic community. George had a great relationship with a Latino professional who also worked at the company. His friend was worried that the escalation of the situation could cause him to lose his job. George handled things skillfully, resulting in the company's taking a new approach to dealing with their Latino stakeholders. Equally important, George resolved the matter in a fashion where his friend not only kept his job but also found his position at the company strengthened through the new policies. George has maintained a deep relationship with his friend because he established a foundation of trust.

Patricia Diaz Dennis advises young Latinos to seek out relationships based on trust and to be savvy about how they develop this trust:

> Find somebody whose judgment you trust and who will respect your confidence. It's usually not somebody at work. This person should show good judgment, and you should feel you can discuss things with them without becoming too vulnerable. Going outside the organization is helpful because people at work can exploit your sharing too much, especially at big companies. Fellow workers can exploit your weakness because everybody is competing for very few jobs at a certain level.

RELATIONSHIPS THAT LAUNCHED A TV SHOW

George Herrera recalls a time when his relationships helped him launch a TV show idea he had, called *Hispanics Today*:

I met with Orlando Padilla, who was at General Motors, and Rudy Beserra, who was at Coca-Cola. I knew Rudy from his days at the White House because I was a delegate to the Reagan-Bush campaign at the national convention, and then Rudy had gone to work for Reagan at the White House. I turned to them right away and said, "I'm trying to get a TV show," and they countered, "TV show?" Next I talked to Jamie Dimon, then the CEO of Bank One and now the CEO of JPMorgan Chase, about the show, and he said, "If you get the TV show, we'd love to advertise on it."

I then returned to NBC with the treatment *and* written sponsorship commitments from General Motors, Coca-Cola, and Bank One. I told the president of NBC New York, Dennis Swanson, "Here's the treatment, and by the way, I've sold all the advertising for the twelve shows if you put me on the air." He replied, "Well, you know what? I like your style, I like your idea, I'm going to put you on the air, and I'm going to put you on the first Sunday of every month after *Meet the Press*."

In September 1998, *Hispanics Today* went on the air on twelve NBC-owned and affiliated stations throughout the country in the top twelve markets. It was seen by twelve million viewers every month.

Hispanics Today became a ratings success, so successful that NBC quickly changed it from a monthly to a weekly show. It highlighted Hispanic leaders like Linda Alvarado, owner of the Colorado Rockies baseball team and founder of a construction firm. The show had a great impact on the broader Latino community because it gave young Hispanics successful role models that they had not seen before on TV.

George's ability to rely on the professional relationships he had established was essential to the creation of *Hispanics Today*— which will be part of his legacy.

SOME RELATIONSHIPS WILL CREATE SPONSORS

Establishing strong relationships makes it more likely that these people will become sponsors who will advocate for you, giving you positive exposure to other executives. They will fight to get you promoted by making sure you are considered for promising and challenging assignments. They will protect you from negative publicity and help you avoid contact with damaging executives.

One of José Armario's sponsors was Jim Skinner, the former CEO of McDonald's. Jim encouraged José to seek a corporate director seat. When a retail bank approached José to serve on their board, Jim advised him that this might not be the best board to join. José listened—and passed on that opportunity. However, he soon joined the board of USG in Chicago, and eventually the board of Avon Products. Based on his ability to build a relationship with the CEO of McDonald's, he encourages young professionals to build relationships with their superiors in the corporate structure.

Early in his career while working at a bank, Lou Nieto established a wonderful relationship with the senior vice president of commercial banking. When the SVP's credit analyst went on a two-week vacation, Lou was asked to fill in temporarily. Lou performed so well that the SVP decided to keep him in that position even after the other person came back from vacation. The person he had replaced had an MBA, while Lou had only completed his undergraduate degree and had just one year's work experience. This gave him an accelerated immersion into the world of commercial banking, and that early break was extremely useful when he later pursued his MBA at Harvard Business School. Most significant was the fact his experience validated the importance of caring about people. In fact, Lou mentions that when ex-employees and coworkers are asked to describe him, "They will say I'm strategic and that I get results, but they always first say that I care about people."

In his book *Good Is Not Enough,*[1] author Keith Wyche talks about the ability to get others to "wear your T-shirt." By this he means that when people walk around bragging about how wonderful they are and all the great things they can do, they are in essence wearing their own T-shirt, often leading to their being seen as braggarts. However, because Latinos and other minorities are less prone to call attention to their accomplishments, they rely more on others to advocate for them—they need others to wear their T-shirt. Through their ability to establish meaningful relationships, transformational Latino leaders get others to wear their T-shirt, and that elevates their chance of career success. Monica Lozano validates this idea:

> Relationships, either in work or outside as it relates to career advancement, are absolutely critical. I've always said your reputation is the one thing that follows you your entire life, and those relationships not only become helpful to you but will also be, in many ways, those that speak for you. When somebody asks, "Can you tell me about so-and-so?" and receives the reply, "She's extraordinary," that's validation.

It's also important to stay in contact with mentors and sponsors, even after leaving a company. While some work relationships may be short, they have the potential to last if you continuously cultivate them. After Victor Arias was accepted into the business school at

Stanford University, his bank president, Art Gonzáles, immediately put him in the company's management program so that he could gain relevant experience before leaving to study for his MBA.

This was extremely valuable for Victor because it provided him with relevant business experience. Before leaving for Stanford, Victor submitted a letter of resignation. However, Art encouraged him to instead request a leave of absence, reminding Victor that he might want to return someday. Even though he had three other job offers after completing his MBA, Victor went back to Texas to work for Art. Victor says having Art as a sponsor was a "godsend." He further explains:

> I think that he saw something, and I was fortunate that he saw that something in me. He was one of those guardian angels you sometimes don't recognize.

When Art's daughter was later going to business school, Victor (who had helped establish the National Society for Hispanic MBAs) made a donation to the school's scholarship fund and allocated the scholarship to Art's daughter, thus further strengthening their relationship. Victor tells others that by building and sustaining relationships, "you find out who has your back."

BUILD MUTUALLY BENEFICIAL RELATIONSHIPS

Another notable approach for building relationships is to establish a reciprocal situation. Our leaders sought relationships not based on what they felt they could gain from the relationship, but with a willingness to give: investing time and energy in other people. They have mastered the art of building relationships because they tend to give as much as they can with no immediate expectation of return in mind. And they often gave more than they received. Patricia Diaz Dennis shares how her willingness to help others has resulted in career opportunities:

When I was a young lawyer, I took a younger lawyer under my wing. I felt sorry for him because he
had nobody when he had moved from the East. He
and I were in the same department, so I invited him
over for dinner, making tacos every Friday night.
He loved my tacos. He eventually gave my name to
someone who then gave my name to presidential
personnel, resulting in President Ronald Reagan
appointing me to the National Labor Relations
Board job. Every single job I've gotten has been because of a friend who recommended me or somebody who knew me.

For Gilbert Casellas, his ability to build and nurture mutually
beneficial relationships has resulted in tremendous career opportunities. His relationship with a fellow trustee for the University
of Pennsylvania helped him secure a spot on the board of directors at Prudential. Later, a friend he met while a member of the
Hispanic Bar Association introduced him to the Clinton administration, leading to his first government appointment. His firsthand
realization of the importance and value of building relationships
is one reason his advice to younger Latinos is so helpful:

I had a partner in my firm in Philadelphia who
said he thought I was a good trial lawyer after I
told him the story of how I grew up and worked in
a family business, a dry-cleaning business belong-
ing to my dad's uncle. I managed the counter all
day, dealing with people of all walks of life. My partner said, "That's why you're a good trial lawyer. You
worked with people of all walks of life. They came
in there, and you treated them well." I said, "Maybe
that's what it is. I don't know if I can answer it any

better." I do try to cultivate relationships. When I talk
to people about networking, the one thing I say is,
"Networking isn't just going to a meeting. It's really
about building relationships. And in building relationships, people want to know that you're there to
give, not just to take."

By nurturing their work relationships generously and consistently,
these leaders avoided what is sometimes called "911 networking":
people reaching out to their network only when they need help or
want something. Those who practice 911 networking are seen as
opportunistic and are quickly labeled as *takers*, not *givers*. They're
seen as manipulative, devious, or just plain selfish. People want to
know that others in a network care about them as a person—not
as a means to an end.

Some Latinos make the error of seeing relationship-building
as playing office politics, acting as if they're above it all. They
believe that their hard work, knowledge, and skills are all that is
required to move up. They lack leadership maturity and have
yet to realize that transformational leaders are highly interde-
pendent individuals who need strong relationships with bosses,
direct reports, senior executives, customers, suppliers, and the
broader community.

ALL BOSSES (THE GOOD, THE BAD, AND THE UGLY) ARE KEY PEOPLE

One of the most important relationships any professional can
build is with their immediate boss. That person evaluates performance, and those ratings have a long-lasting influence on career
success. Patricia Diaz Dennis reminds others: "It is absolutely
critical to maintain a strong relationship with one's boss." Jorge
Figueredo, retired executive vice president at McKesson, also

encourages those with a bad boss to still maintain a good relationship with them:

> Even when you have a bad boss, you can learn so much from them. First, you can learn what not to do when you become a boss. Second, rarely are bosses bad 100 percent of the time, so learn from them while you can, because bad bosses don't tend to stick around too long.

Monica Lozano adds that another way of dealing with a bad boss is to simply excel at work. She states:

> Create allies and find sponsors when you have a bad boss. Identify other sponsors in the organization, but first demonstrate really high levels of performance. Never let yourself be put on your hind feet because you didn't perform at the very highest levels.

As we can see, the benefits of being able to manage relationships effectively are many and varied. The key distinction for our transformational Latino leaders is that relationship-building was not considered additional work—it *was* the work.

From Being to Doing

These first three keys to success—embracing ambition, taking risks, and investing in relationships—are traits, dispositions of how to *be*. Transformative leaders demonstrate key differentiating competencies as well—the necessary action-oriented skills and behaviors. In the case of our Latino executives, these are (1) being politically savvy about how to navigate corporate culture, (2) establishing and shaping one's own leadership style, and (3) paying it forward by giving back to the community—topics we turn to in the next chapter.

BUILDING LATINO TALENT INSIDE AND OUTSIDE THE ORGANIZATIONAL WALLS

Lou Miramontes, a retired partner at KPMG, provides an excellent example of just how transformational leaders go about making a difference in the Latino community. Shortly after being named a partner, he recalls this scenario:

> When I returned to the U.S. practice after a foreign assignment in Latin America, I observed that there weren't a lot of Latino leaders in corporate America. You hear they don't have the skill or they don't have the contacts so they don't know how to navigate situations. I said to myself, and I told people, "You're absolutely nuts. I just spent five years in Latin America dealing with some of the most savvy, successful Hispanics, and they got it. They had good success, and they are thriving, so it has nothing to do with the color of our skin or our last name. It has to do with opportunity, and it has to do with getting those folks to go into the mainstream.

Lou went on a mission to change KPMG, developing a strategy to bring in more Latinos. He convinced the CEO and the chairman of the business case for more Latino partners due to accelerating international and Latin American business growth. After getting their buy-in, he developed an internal network with the handful of other Latino partners. Understanding that these Latinos needed guidance, he secured mentors and sponsors to teach them how the business really works, how decisions are made, how to secure budgets for initiatives—in short, how the corporate culture operates. Over a ten-year period, they successfully recruited and promoted a record number of Latinos.

Lou's realization of the need for more Latinos had compelled him to make a positive impact. He also took his mission of growing Latino talent outside the firm's walls. He decided he wanted to help increase the overall number of Latinos going into the fields of accounting and finance. He became actively involved in the Latino nonprofit ALPFA. For years, he has helped to secure jobs for Latino graduates with big firms, helped raise scholarship funds for bright Latino students, and raised awareness within the larger Latino community of the benefits of working at accounting and finance firms.

Now a director on a corporate board, Lou is a member of the Latino Corporate Directors Association (LCDA), which helps to secure board seats for Latino executives. It's no surprise that he is joined as a member of the LCDA by other transformational Latino leaders highlighted in this book, including José Armario, Victor Arias, Gilbert Casellas, Patricia Diaz Dennis, Cari Dominguez, Charlie Garcia, Grace Lieblein, Monica Lozano, Lou Nieto, Darren Rebelez, and Luis Ubiñas—to name just a few.

CHAPTER 7

What to Do: Three Key Competencies of Transformational Leaders

Cuestionar tu propio proceso es una necesidad.
Si no te cuestionas a ti mismo, es imposible mejorar.

To question your own process is a necessity. If you don't question
yourself, it's impossible to improve.

—Alejandro González Iñárritu, Mexican film director

We have delved into the three traits of becoming a transformative leader: embracing ambition as an honorable intent, taking risks as a catalyst for growth and getting noticed, and valuing relationships deeply. Now let's examine the three competencies, the skills and the abilities that emerged as necessities:

- Political savvy about corporate culture
- Ability to establish and shape your own leadership style
- Giving back to the community

We believe that there is a developmental sequence to these three competencies.

First, individuals must learn to master the politics that determine how to advance within the corporate culture. When trying to break into the leadership ranks, they cannot survive very long without this skill. Yet there is a delicate balance here: authentic leaders will recognize the warning signs of nearing the danger zone of compromising their own uniqueness and of losing themselves by hewing too closely to corporate norms.

Once transformative leaders have established their credibility and relationships within the system, they don't just stay with the pack; rather, they find ways to differentiate themselves from others. By doing so, they begin to formulate and shape their unique leadership style. Having mastered the cultural customs of the corporation, they know when and where to break the rules. The Latino executive who has done the foundational work of being authentically grounded in their cultural identity can now identify outlets through which their diverse views and behaviors can flow outward, and in so doing, differentiate their leadership.

Finally, after leaders have accumulated a followership, career accomplishments and recognition, and financial success, they are strategically placed to generously share their time, resources, and sponsorship.

Let's take a deeper dive into each of these competencies.

Political Savvy About Corporate Culture

When an ambitious person comes from a traditionally underrepresented group, any organization's unique corporate culture poses a formidable challenge to securing a place in the top echelons. Why? As we saw in chapter 4, Latino and corporate American cultures can clash in profound ways. Because corporate America was founded by European-American men who established their norms for business based on what worked best for them, it follows that this confers advantages for them and disadvantages for those who do not have the same cultural legacy.

Being able to decipher and follow a company's culture is an all-encompassing endeavor because the culture defines particular ways to think, speak, and act within the company. Those who don't follow established ways are seen as not fitting in. Those individuals who do break through by delivering the expected results tend to be successful, and that success leads to greater leadership roles. Those leaders then reinforce the existing culture in which they have triumphed, through a variety of mechanisms such as allocating resources, giving rewards, and doling out punishments.

Transformative leaders go further to influence changes in the culture. For leaders and companies committed to becoming more diverse and inclusive, cultural changes are needed, because the legacy culture's norms actively reinforce the glass ceiling that few minorities can break through. Before anyone can achieve a position with enough power to influence cultural changes, they must first have an intimate knowledge of the culture and become successful at navigating within it.

How can you master corporate culture without losing your own sense of identity? That is the challenge. Following are some of the leaders' insights:

BE A STUDENT OF CORPORATE CULTURE

Former Bank of America executive Cari Dominguez told us:

> Understanding the unwritten rules at work is more valuable than the written rules. Everyone knows

the official rules, but only a few really understand the unwritten ones.

Through keen observation of what was happening around them, the Latino leaders in our study figured out the unwritten rules. José Armario, the former McDonald's executive and Avon board member, explains how he picked up cues on how people advanced within McDonald's corporate structure:

> I carefully observed how some approached promotions. I liked how they did it in terms of a balanced, professional, fact-driven way, and I tried to emulate that. But I also saw the political ugliness of an executive team where some people are jockeying for time, always have something to say, and are "besties" with the boss (or try to be) in ways that can influence decisions along the way.
>
> If you observe, you pick up the good and try to emulate but stay wary of some of the other not-so-positive intentions that people may have. Some people move up the ladder because they've made the right connections; they hit it off with people. Their work has been okay, but they have the confidence of the person in charge. They survive, but eventually the cream does rise to the top. You do get exposed for who you really are, the higher up you go. In the corporate culture, if you didn't know your stuff you got exposed quite easily. I saw some people fail when they got exposed, while those who were knowledgeable and fact-driven, and knew their responsibilities, typically not just survived, but thrived.

Even the most seasoned corporate executives are sometimes thrust into environments where they must quickly determine the corporate culture. Forcepoint executive Myrna Soto tells how she learned this lesson very early in her career in a customer service role, and it served her well as she made her way to the top:

> Early in my career I was at this company with a very unique corporate culture: a privately owned family company, headquartered in Miami, but with roots in Norway and Eastern Europe. There I was, a Hispanic in Miami, and, I'll admit, a little loud and boisterous. I was initially not welcomed since I was not really what they wanted. While they wanted results, discipline, and hard work, they were very reserved. You talked when you were spoken to, so I learned what it would take to be able to navigate and grow within the company by respecting some of the corporate cultural norms. However, I still challenged procedures, asked many questions, and contributed ideas about how the call center was being run. Because of this combined approach, I quickly ascended to a management role.

At first Myrna's dual approach of playing by the corporate norms but still offering her break-the-mold ideas was rewarded by the culture because she achieved results. But soon enough she began to hear that her style had its limits and was not always appreciated by everyone within the company:

> Because I was this young whippersnapper who had just graduated from college and was learning about their operations, I'm saying, "God, we should be doing this and we should be doing that, and this and that and blah, blah, blah." There was a point

in time where some of the leaders above me said, "Hey, you know, settle down, because every time we have a meeting you're always kind of like…whatever [outspoken]." Even in a culture where my ideas weren't necessarily welcomed, it was impossible for me to restrain myself 100 percent. I think I learned over time how to better nuance my adaptation to the culture without losing my distinctive voice. I learned how to introduce my ideas and how to respectfully challenge the status quo by saying, "I hear what you say, but I believe that you should consider what I'm sharing with you."

And it worked. As I ascended to more senior roles, I was provided the platform and the opportunity to be able to take very distinct stances on certain topics and issues. If I look back and ask, "Would I have had as much courage as an entry-level worker in a particular place to take the stances I took later on as I ascended to more senior roles?" I'm not so sure.

Later, when she left that company to join American Express, Myrna discovered another cultural transition she needed to make:

I moved from wearing semi-casual, business casual in Miami, to the corporate power suit at American Express. These are rules that nobody explains to you, but when you enter the environment you quickly realize *Oh, I'm not fitting in.*

As much as there can be tensions between archetypal Latino and corporate American cultures, there are many individual Latino leaders who find that their personalities and inner drivers naturally gravitate toward the corporate culture. For example, Lou Miramontes's personal work style aligned perfectly with the culture at the accounting firm KPMG. This not only helped him fit in but also gave him a competitive advantage in the aggressive work environments of professional services firms, where people are vying for a limited number of partnerships.

> I learned the keys to success. The first was that you had to be willing to work crazy hours during busy seasons. But I was used to working long hours and getting up early. That was easy; my dad did it, rising at 4 a.m. to go to a factory. In contrast, I had the privilege of putting a suit on and going to an office. That ethic of work was with me, setting me apart from the pack. I was able to work and learn how to serve clients and develop relationships.

Later, Lou came to see the value of performance evaluations as another way to gain insights on how to be successful within the KPMG culture:

> Performance evaluations pointed out to me the tasks I did well. Those evaluations were also very blunt about what I did not do well. Having both sides of the table come at me in a constructive way was really helpful. Sometimes there were criticisms that were tough to hear: "Hey you're superficial; you didn't follow up," or "You have to be more visible." Bottom line: you have to have a cultural learning component to your professional life.

ONCE YOU LEARN THE CORPORATE CULTURE, USE YOUR LEADERSHIP POSITION TO CHANGE IT

Patricia Diaz Dennis recalls being on the National Labor Relations Board when she had her third child. Because of her role as a leader, Patricia felt it was important to shift the culture to be more supportive of parents and to have family-friendly policies. She also saw that leaders needed to lead by example.

> I realized I needed to be what I wanted the change to be. So I brought my newborn daughter Alicia to the office, and I nursed her there. Then I let the women on my staff—I had a staff of twenty-one lawyers—know that if they needed time for family-related reasons or if they were going to come in late or leave early, it was all okay. When you're a professional, doing your work on a flexible schedule is acceptable; that you do get your work done is the important issue.

For some of our Latino executives, having key decision-making roles at their company helped them see how things really got done behind the curtain—including practices that were unfair. Cari Dominguez recalls being confronted with this reality when she had a leadership role in human resources at a major banking institution:

> I was responsible for the care and feeding of the top two hundred executives—compensation, executive recruitment and benefits, developmental assignments, executive education—anything that had to do with the top executives. It was a one-stop shop so the executives wouldn't have to go through each other or go through any complicated processes. They would simply go through me. I had my own team who worked with the chairman and the vice chairman, making sure that these executives were well taken care of: bonuses, equity, different perks. But it became clear that there were really no criteria for who received the perks and who didn't. I kept

wondering why did some get it, while these others didn't? It was quite the subjective process.

Not surprisingly, this led to her recognizing that the culture at this organization favored certain groups over others. Men enjoyed international assignments, executive education programs, and other opportunities for which women were not seriously considered—which gave them an edge when it came time for promotions and increased pay. Cari felt the culture needed to change.

> As people moved up the ladder, they became part of a much more subjective process when being considered for the rewards, the transfers, the assignments. Since I felt very strongly about how these things were happening, I went to the chairman and said, "We've got issues. There are invisible barriers here concerning the advancement of people." The CEO was quite shocked because he was a very progressive individual who had three daughters. He said, "I want everyone to feel included, so let's do a study." He commissioned me to do an upward-mobility review, and I was able to brief him and the whole management committee about the findings. We made structural changes to the process after the conclusion of the study.

Knowing how the inner workings and company culture at an institution can limit upward mobility for women was pivotal for Cari, leading her to decide she needed a broader platform from which to heighten awareness of issues of disparity and inequity. She would soon be called upon by then Secretary of Labor Elizabeth Dole to take a role with her political team, and eventually she became the chair of the U.S. Equal Employment Opportunity Commission.

> I wanted to use this platform for public policy-making to really make companies accountable for the progression, the advancement, the inclusion, and the parity of treatment for all their employees. That's where the Glass Ceiling Initiative began. We developed a final project and met with the policy council and the White House. President George H. W. Bush at the time actually used talking points we had drafted in one of his presidential debates. It was a highly accepted initiative. To this day I have women coming up to me and saying that as a result of all that public policy-making work, they got an opportunity within the company to advance and to move into nontraditional areas.

Through a thorough understanding of how corporate culture works to the benefit of a privileged few and against most others, Cari was able to leverage that insight to make positive, transformational change—not just within a particular company, but nationwide.

As Latinos strive for more C-suite roles, they have to be able to not only understand corporate culture, but also change and shape it.

Ability to Establish and Shape Your Leadership Style

Our successful Latino executives' leadership styles were consistently shaped from values, character, and experiences forged in the crucible of their formative years, when family, culture, institutions, and personality were all defining influences. Many characteristics of their leadership styles would have been apparent early in their careers, and likely were more generic: discipline, hard work, accomplishing tasks, and inspiring others to follow them.

But the characteristics of their differentiated leadership styles—those actions that may run counter to the corporate culture—often did not fully manifest until they had unraveled that culture and the politics behind it. In essence, the culture grants grudging permission to be challenged—only after deference has been paid to it.

Let's look first at the power of the formative years in shaping leaders, and then at those moments of truth when the transformative leader breaks the existing paradigms.

THE ESSENCE OF THE PERSON BECOMES THE ESSENCE OF THE LEADER

Former GameStop CEO Paul Raines acknowledges that his leadership style was deeply influenced by his upbringing in Costa Rica and close connection with his family:

> My Latin heritage plays a huge part in what I've done in my career and with my leadership style. As a leader and as an executive in any organization, I've approached things as a family more than I would have had I not had that experience of being born and raised in Costa Rica. Our motto here at GameStop is "Protect the family." That's how we define our reason for being.

By invoking a leadership style that creates a family environment, Paul's approach ripples far beyond the workplace. He told us, "I get letters and emails from people I've met twenty-five years ago, and they still remember me.

Another way that Paul's approach transcends normal workplace boundaries is his deep commitment to helping others be successful—which serves as another foundational component of his leadership style. He states:

> Maybe it relates to my Catholic upbringing. I have found that you get a lot further by helping people around you be successful than by always trying to stand out by yourself. And you'll find aiding others makes you successful over time.

Even though Paul describes his philosophy as being a servant leader, fiercely focused on helping others and rooted in family, that does not mean he has a soft approach. He relies on accountability and developing a reputation for excellence to round out his leadership style.

> Looking in the mirror for accountability is extremely important. Bad leaders look in the mirror when things are going well and congratulate themselves, and good leaders look in the mirror and ask, "What am I going to do different today to try to make the situation better?" You have to develop a reputation for excellence in everything you do. There's no room for excuses. The last job I had to be interviewed for was my first job after coming out of school. Ever since then I've been pulled along by people I knew, people I met, and relationships I built. Excellence in everything you do is very important. You can't be mediocre.

Darren Rebelez, CEO of Casey's General Stores, says his leadership style was solidified by his experiences attending West Point, the U.S. military academy. He recalls West Point as being extremely challenging from an academic standpoint, but he loved the environment because of the esprit de corps and the sense of purpose. He describes what it was like:

You're there to go to school, but it wasn't just going to school. West Point is really a leadership school, cloaked in a college. You were there to train, to become a leader, and to be prepared to help defend the nation if called upon. I went there from '84 to '88. The Cold War was still in full swing, and the Soviet Union still existed. So we were training for a potentially very large, conventional war. My best friends in the world today are the people I went to school with there.

Darren tells how his leadership style was further defined by his military experience:

I was really excited about getting into the Army, and after four years of training and education, I became an infantry officer, a paratrooper, and an Army ranger. It was a really good experience. I was taught about leadership and practiced leadership by being placed in charge of people. When I think about the level of responsibility that I had as a new lieutenant who's twenty-two or twenty-three years old, it's quite a staggering thought. My first job was as a platoon leader, where I had forty men I was responsible for. Then shortly after being promoted, my unit was deployed to the Gulf War. I was twenty-five years old, leading 120 soldiers, and responsible for millions of dollars in vehicles and equipment. I had to take them halfway around the world for a fight. The level of responsibility I was given and the leadership challenges I faced were not like anything I would get in corporate America, certainly at that stage of my career.

When asked how his West Point education and military career impacted his leadership style, Darren stated:

> My military career is central to how I approach things. I learned that 80 percent of leadership is showing up. You just can't mail it in if you're going to be a leader. You have to be there, on the ground, with your people. In the infantry, we have a saying that you have to lead from the front, especially when things get a little dicey and the soldiers are looking for you to show them what to do. So I've always viewed leadership as a hands-on exercise.
>
> Even today, in my job as CEO of Casey's General Stores, I get out and visit stores. It never ceases to amaze me that people are so impressed that I, as CEO of the company, actually show up and sit down to have conversations with the people who work there. It's such a simple thing, but it means so much to people and builds confidence in them and trust between them and their leaders. They should expect more out of a leader than just showing up, but that's the way it is.
>
> Another principle that I learned at West Point is doing the harder right versus the easier wrong. That's actually something that's in the cadet prayer. I always think about this because it's simple to take the easy way out. But as leaders we're held to a higher standard, and that oftentimes means making difficult decisions. The only way anybody's ever going to follow you is if they trust you, and the only way to build that trust is through demonstrating character and integrity.

When Darren decided to leave the military and pursue a corporate career, he relied heavily on his military leadership experience. He recalls interviewing with PepsiCo during this transition.

> I said, "Look, I don't know much about this business, but the one thing I do know is if you give me a group of people I can get stuff done." They said, "OK, we've got a job like that in our restaurant business."

True to his word, this leadership style eventually took Darren all the way to becoming the president of a restaurant chain.

Five Below's Juan Galarraga feels that two very different aspects of his life greatly influenced his leadership style: being an immigrant, which instilled in him a relentless work ethic, and realizing he wasn't as great at soccer as he had thought he was. He explains that as a youth growing up in Venezuela, he excelled at soccer, often as the best player on the team. But when he came to college in the U.S. on a soccer scholarship, he soon realized he was no longer one of the best players on the team. This required him to shift his playing style to focus more on teamwork and team success as opposed to personal success. He credits this emphasis on establishing high-performing teams as a key to his career success.

US Hispanic Media Group Board Chair Monica Lozano says her approach to leadership was shaped by a variety of experiences growing up, including being an activist as a student at the University of Oregon:

> I joined in the César Chávez boycotts in solidarity with the United Farm Workers. We were boycotting the student union because they were serving non-union lettuce. We'd get up at five in the morning and make sandwiches to sell in front of the student union. UFW were boycotting Safeway stores, so we

would choose a store to picket. There was also a big vote on campus to divest from investments in South Africa to protest apartheid there. It was the first time I had been a part of student activism. They were issues I could relate to on a personal level.

Those days of activism started Monica on a course that led to her becoming the publisher of *La Opinión*, the largest Spanish-language newspaper in the U.S., providing a daily platform for the needs, wants, and aspirations of the Latino community.

SEIZING THE MOMENTS OF TRUTH TO FORGE A DIFFERENTIATED LEADERSHIP STYLE

Here are two moment-of-truth stories from leaders we interviewed. For each one of them, it would be a watershed moment—a milestone in the forging of their leadership styles.

Monica Lozano tells the first story. She clearly remembers a very difficult moment of truth that went a long way in defining her leadership style. The family-owned newspaper she was leading was facing an existential crisis. Given many social, economic, and media trends, the Latino newspaper needed to (ironically, given many of the themes in this book) change from a familial culture to a more professional one in order to remain relevant. Media segmentation was completely transforming the media landscape. After sixty years of having a great brand in a region where Spanish-language television and radio were quite parochial—and had little competition—suddenly there was competition everywhere, including from emerging powerhouses such as Telemundo and Univision. She explains how they rose to the challenge in spite of great personal anguish:

> As much as we valued the deep personal relationships, we needed to shift the culture of the company.

We were repositioning *La Opinión* from being a Latino-owned business to being an American institution and to demand our rightful place in U.S. society. We had to demand excellence from everybody and drive accountability throughout the organization. We went through a significant process of articulating a vision and evaluating where we stood against that vision, building our internal competencies, and developing the kind of external relationships that are required to succeed in this business. At the end of the day we needed to monetize all of this to have a revenue stream that was going to support our dreams.

In the end, Monica helped to successfully elevate the organization to the next level. But it took strong leadership to do it. As she describes, when transformational leaders chart the course for others and for the organization, they bring culture change while still finding ways to retain cultural elements that could carry over to the new reality:

My orientation toward leadership is very collaborative. I really believe in empowering teams; I believe in delegating. You get the best and the brightest around you, and then successfully communicate the passion and the possibility of what can be. The responsibility can't be the responsibility of just one person. It has to include the entire organization.

You can only win if you can create a culture that empowers a company and all of the people who work there to want to win with you. I'm very hands on, very much about managing by walking around and getting to know the people on the team. I

would try to meet every new employee: "Come in
and let me tell you why we want you here, what I'm
expecting of you. If you ever need me, I'm here." I
don't know if that's a Latino style or just my style.
I learned it from my dad. He was very accessible.
You don't want to lose the essence of the spirit of
the business.

Charlie Garcia tells the second story. In addition to the numerous leadership roles he's held, he has written two books related
to leadership. In 2003, he wrote *A Message from Garcia: Yes, You
Can Succeed*. He tells the following moment-of-truth story, which
involves the Supreme Court, Colin Powell, Governor Jeb Bush,
and President George W. Bush:

When I was on the Board of Education in Florida,
the issue of affirmative action at the University of
Michigan had come before the Supreme Court.
Colin Powell issued a short press release saying
that he strongly supported affirmative action. Both
President George W. Bush and Governor Jeb Bush
submitted briefs against the University of Michigan.
I found out a group of Fortune 500 CEOs were sub
mitting a brief to the U.S. Supreme Court in support of affirmative action, and I decided to join that
brief. When I called the lawyer handling the brief,
he said, "Hell, who are you? You've got this small
company, and this is a Fortune 500 brief." Then they
found out I was on the state board of education and
working for the president on the Air Force Academy
board, so I became a signatory to that brief. Well,
my action really upset the governor who I was working for in Florida, Jeb Bush.

I was also in the doghouse with the president of the United States and his staff. The Supreme Court decision came out in favor of affirmative action, with Sandra Day O'Connor writing the majority opinion. I went to see the president at an event in Crawford, Texas. I said, "Mr. President, I hope you remember what Ronald Reagan said." "What's that?" "When someone is your friend 80 percent of the time, they're your friend." He laughed. As I was about to leave, he put his hand on my shoulder, turned me around, and I remember thinking *Wow, he's pretty strong for an old guy*. But he stuck out his hand and said, "Charlie, I want to thank you for serving my administration and thank you for standing up for what you believe in."

The very next week an important White House policy giving special consideration to Latinos was being discussed, but before they announced the new policy, they wanted my input—which had never happened before.

Giving Back to the Community

Giving back to the community requires the trait of a generous spirit, combined with the competence to do it well. The arc of the transformative Latino executive is not complete until the accomplishments of executives have elevated and inspired them to better the lives and prospects of individuals and groups outside their corporate world. In contrast to the business world's reciprocal, transactional nature of exchanging many tangible, extrinsic benefits, giving back to the community is more an act of generosity that does not expect or demand anything in return.

Those who have accumulated power, wealth, and influence can then use these assets as leverage on behalf of others who may need an extra lift to seize opportunities just beyond their reach. Transformational Latino leaders also realize that if they don't become involved in the process of making a difference and clearing the way for more Latinos to come through, they can't complain about the lack of a Latino pipeline.

The Latino executive also carries an additional burden to give back, since there are so few Latino corporate executives who can be tapped for help. They are constantly being called on to support Latino and other diversity initiatives. The executives we interviewed have all responded to this call. In many cases they were the first wave of Latinos at their corporations, and for much of their careers they labored alone to disprove stereotypes. They had to learn how to read unspoken messages, spot danger signals, and overcome obstacles. They were ready for the hard work of being the first or the only Latino in the company. They knew that their successes and failures would be considered as representative of their Hispanic ethnicity. Because of this labeling, they are determined that the next generation of Latino leaders will not be as alone as they were. The need is so great that many expressed anxiety about not being able to do enough.

Myrna Soto believes wholeheartedly that this giving back is a key responsibility of transformational Latino leaders:

> All my Latino brothers and sisters out there with similar stature as me need to help other Latinos. I also believe in HITEC's [Hispanic IT Executive Council] vision and mission, which is that we need to push and pull each other up to higher levels every time we have an opportunity.

Juan Galarraga recalls that an obligation to help others was always part of his leadership style, but the seriousness of it really kicked in when he was promoted to a vice president position at a very young age:

> There was a point in time when I started to realize that I needed to be part of something bigger than myself. That's when I started to fall in love with the idea of paving the way for others, specifically Hispanics, and not just at Target, but within the broader Hispanic community. I realized that I would have never been given those chances if I didn't have the right mentors and/or sponsors throughout my career, and I realized that I was being looked up to as a role model by a lot of team members.

> For years I've been very involved with the Hispanic Association on Corporate Responsibility [HACR], which is where I started the Hispanic Executive Forum. Then I was blessed to join the board of the Hispanic Scholarship Fund, an organization that builds the foundations toward education for the Hispanic community. I am passionate about this work and would not feel complete as a leader if I did not give back this way.

While giving back with maximum power and influence becomes easier as leaders achieve the highest levels, the discipline and practice of giving back should begin early in Latino leaders' careers. For example, Gilbert Casellas's commitment to making a difference began early in his life, deeply rooted in his family's history with the mutual aid societies and social clubs back in Tampa.

Gilbert, the current board director at Prudential Insurance, started making an impact while an undergrad student at Yale University. Noticing the relatively few Latino students at Yale, he first established a successful Latino student organization. Next he secured funds from a foundation to establish the first Puerto Rican cultural center on campus. Eventually he became involved in demonstrations against the ineffective ways that Yale was recruiting Latino students. Soon Gilbert was meeting with the president of the university. He eventually helped Yale establish a better Latino recruiting strategy, resulting in a substantial increase of Latino students. That set the stage for a lifetime of lifting up Latino talent throughout his career at law firms and law schools, and in government, the military, and corporate America. Each time he did so on a greater scale and with more sustainable results.

Across the country at Stanford, Victor Arias was playing a similar role. After building a strong connection with Dr. Jerry Porras, coauthor of the book *Built to Last: Successful Habits of Visionary Companies*, Victor started Latino business student organizations, which ultimately led to his becoming one of the founding members of the National Society of Hispanic MBAs.

For Lisa Garcia Quiroz, the Harvard alum, her role in making a difference included helping other Latino students be accepted into Harvard. She was actively involved in the undergraduate minority student recruitment program, working in the admissions office for three years advocating for Latino students. She was so involved and made such an impact, the *Harvard Crimson* published a profile of her, calling her "the Godmother to her Community." She remained actively involved, helping Latino students by serving as the chair for the national Hispanic Scholarship Fund.

Luis Ubiñas also began making a difference early in his career. He joined his first nonprofit board in Boston when he was only in his mid-twenties. Then, after a successful nineteen-year career at the consulting firm McKinsey & Company, he left and joined Ford Foundation as its president so he could give back on a significantly larger scale.

José Armario felt it was his obligation to increase the number of Latino leaders at McDonald's:

> I was fortunate that McDonald's already had a strong commitment to diversity, but we were tasked to find the time and ways to strengthen the Latino networks at the corporation, to put together plans to present to the head of HR or the COO or CEO, plans of how to help grow Hispanic succession and pipelines. There were constant discussions about these initiatives. As I rose in influence, I also became more influential in accelerating and strengthening the pipeline of Latino leaders at McDonald's. I always tell people I mentor: "Somebody did you a favor along the way. You now have to do the same. You need to pay it forward because if it stops with you, then we all lose."

These transformational Latino leaders who understand the power and obligation of giving back, and who are skilled at doing so, do not hesitate to ask other Latinos in positions of authority, "What has your contribution to Latino advancement been?" Their answers will speak volumes.

Purpose-Driven Leadership

As we wrap up these two chapters of the three key traits and the three key competencies of transformational Latino leaders, we must note one final characteristic that pulls these elements together: being a purpose-driven leader. Former AT&T executive Patricia

Diaz Dennis believes this strongly—that having a purpose provides a compass for a person's actions and career decisions:

> Most people think that leadership is something positional, such as being a CEO or a CFO or general counsel. For me, ultimately, it's about something very different. It's about leading your life with purpose. Think about where you want to go, what you want to accomplish, what impact you want to have in the world, and then devise a plan and ultimately follow that plan. Don't get cast about—take control.

When asked to describe her purpose, Patricia doesn't hesitate:

> My purpose is to inspire, serve, and connect others to achieve extraordinary things. I want to make life better for the people who are with me on this journey, as well as the people who come after.

Inspired? Hopefully you are. In our next chapter, we'll tackle one more leadership topic, one that many Latino professionals tend to struggle with: power.

CHAPTER 8

Power Ambivalence: The Achilles Heel

Lavarse las manos del conflicto entre los medios poderosos y los impotentes al lado de los poderosos, no es ser neutral.

Washing one's hands of the conflict between the powerful and the powerless means to side with the powerful, not to be neutral.

—Paulo Freire, Brazilian educator and philosopher

So far, our exploration of Latino executive success has been a story of onward and upward. The leaders we interviewed have been inspirational. They have overcome a myriad of societal and organizational biases by optimizing their resilience, hard work, and ambition, as well as by coming to terms with their cultural identity.

However, in our research we saw a consistent uncomfortable theme that could be one of the root causes of why the Latino presence in executive leadership in corporate America has been

stuck at 5 percent for too many years. While we have documented various root causes anchored in systemic discrimination,
unconscious biases, and inflexible corporate cultures, there is at
least one cause within Latino culture that could be at play as
well: a deep-seated ambivalence toward the concept, practice,
and pursuit of power.

Clearly, Latinos have power in numbers. Being the largest ethnic
minority in the U.S., at 18.5 percent of the population, they have
an annual purchasing power of $1.7 trillion, which is growing by
around $100 billion a year. They have political power too, with an
ability to tip elections as they did during Barack Obama's victories
in 2008 and 2012. This kind of impact proves that this once-
marginalized minority is on a path to demographic relevance.

Yet it is a suboptimized power. In the 2016 presidential election,
many assumed Donald Trump's vitriolic rhetoric against Latinos
would unleash a bang of Latino electoral resistance. Instead,
Latino power ended in a whimper, as they did not play a deci-
sive role in the outcome by turning up to vote as much as they
needed to. True before Trump's election—and even truer after-
ward—Latino social, educational, and health needs remain near
the bottom of government priorities. These shortcomings show
that even though Latinos are in a demographic boom and have
more money to spend, their ability as a collective force to wield
power and gain influence is still somewhat meek and muted.

Then, in the 2020 election, Latinos did begin to have their presence
felt in more measurable ways, yet we did so by pulling in opposite directions politically: toward Biden in Arizona, Georgia, and
Wisconsin, and toward Trump in Florida and Texas.

This suboptimization of power also plays out among Latinos in
their careers. Though we interviewed twenty of perhaps the most

powerful Latinos in corporate America, we had difficulty finding a compelling or well-defined approach to how Latinos can individually and collectively increase their power in their work environments. When the topic was broached, we detected a consistent desire to pivot to another subject, and when it came to the topic of power, their remarks expressed ambivalence.

Our Latino executives' relationship with power seemed to be ancillary. For example, several commented that power was achieved only after the pursuit of something more positive. For Jorge Figueredo, the retired executive vice president for HR at McKesson, gaining power takes an indirect route: "I don't make having more power the goal. I focus on other issues and power will come." Similarly, when asked about power, Diversified Search's Victor Arias shared, "I have a negative connotation of power only because power suggests that rather than trying to influence others to do the right thing, you are trying to force them to do the right thing."

Southwest Airlines board member Grace Lieblein has had a very successful career in corporate America, yet she had this to say about her relationship to power:

> I probably gave away more power than I tried to take. Power to me was not something I had to go grab. I always felt like the more power you give away, the more it comes back to you at some point. Sounds like a Zen philosopher, I know. I'm really not a power player. It goes back to my not being political. Instead I have a position. I ran GM Mexico, I ran GM Brazil. I used power as a part of those jobs but used it appropriately. I just never thought in the vein of having to gain more power, of having to attain a bigger position, or get more, more, more. That's just not who I am.

GameStop's former CEO Paul Raines observed:

> When it comes to power, I'm a contrarian. I don't see the word *power* as a real word that I use and talk about very much. There's definitely power in organizations, and I'm often confused when I read about concentration of power in case studies or in publications such as the *Wall Street Journal*. I just don't see the world that way.
>
> I'm trying to have more of a servant-leadership mentality than the other way around. Maybe I think that power comes from the base and it's an inverse pyramid. I see my relationship with power as more of being a servant to the power of the customer than anything else. I've always believed that if you do a great job on what you're working on today and establish a reputation for excellence, the power issue takes care of itself.

This hesitancy to speak directly about power and their relationship with it seemed significant to us. So we decided to compare how our Latino leaders discussed the topic of power against the discourse of a group of executives from another racial/ethnic minority group: African Americans.

In the philosophy that from a diversity of backgrounds, experiences, and culture there are lessons to be learned that can benefit other groups, what can Latinos learn from the Black approach to power? As you will see, the contrast is stark. It surfaces questions of whether Latinos are leaving some power on the table due to their ambivalence, and if so, how they can optimize power and yet stay true to a Latino ethos.

One final caveat: Clearly the Latino executives we interviewed are high achievers and successful leaders with exemplary track records—all characteristics of using the power of their positions, being able to articulate a vision, developing a followership, and achieving results. However, it's the ambivalence toward this power that intrigued us. In a world with massive forces holding back broader Latino achievement, is there a deeper reservoir of power that Latino leaders could be tapping into to exponentially amplify the positive impact they are already displaying?

Compare and Contrast, a Case Study: African-American Executives and Power

Authors Price Cobbs and Judith Turnock provide a comprehensive examination of the relationship that successful African-American executives have with power in the workplace. Their book, *Cracking the Corporate Code*,[1] based on stories from thirty-two Black corporate executives, declares that if African Americans do not grasp the essence of power's importance, they will never have real power in corporations. In our own review of their relationship with power, we found that not only are African-American executives more comfortable than Latino executives discussing power, they are more comfortable actively pursuing it.

Cobbs and Turnock describe four key realities of corporate life that African-American leaders have come to understand. First, they agree that within an organizational context, power involves conflict and disagreement. Second, for those who aspire to positions of influence, a critical personal attribute is the willingness to engage in conflict with others. Third, African Americans recognize that whether stated openly or not, every organizational transaction is a statement of who has and who does not have power. Finally, there's an acknowledgment that unless African-American executives know what to do with power when they have it, they will squander it.

The acceptance of these four realities clearly demonstrates a strong embrace of power, as well as a level of comfort with the conflict associated with it. What has led African Americans in the U.S. to this very different relationship to power compared to Latinos? The answers lie in comparing and contrasting how the different contours of the Black and Latino experiences led to different philosophies about interacting with power, different leadership role models, and different institutional responses—all of which have led to different outcomes.

We can distill why these two communities emerged with different points of view around power by looking at Black and Latino experiences through these three lenses:

- Affinity through experience
- Faith and religion
- Educational, not-for-profit, and political institutions

AFFINITY THROUGH EXPERIENCE

Both Blacks and Latinos in the U.S. have suffered greatly from prejudice and discrimination. Oppression, pain, and death were often delivered by similar means. Other dimensions of the violence against these two groups were manifested differently due to different historical circumstances. European Americans brought Black slaves by force to the Americas. Mexicans were driven from their own land after the Mexican-American War. Blacks faced slavery. Latinos faced indentured servitude. Blacks were brought in chains; Latinos even today are deported in chains or detained in immigration cages.

However, there are fundamental differences in the systems of oppression that Blacks and Latinos endured. These differences had a distinctive impact on how both groups came to understand the power of affinity through skin color and a shared experience.

While Latino subjugation was fragmented across the U.S., Black subjugation was systemic. The institution of slavery was part of a massive, cohesive economic system dependent on unpaid labor that powered the American South. Southern society was structured around slavery and its ancillary repercussions. It lasted more than two hundred years, and to demolish it required a civil war in which more than 620,000 Americans died.

Given its systemic nature, Blacks had a more uniform history of their oppression compared to Latinos, whose tyranny varied depending on where in the U.S. it happened, the socioeconomics of the populace, and their immigration status. By its very nature, the crucible of slavery and, after that, the Jim Crow laws, made a deep and broad shared experience—and therefore a strong affinity among Blacks—inevitable.

In contrast, there has not been one massive oppressive unifying experience for all Latinos as there was for Blacks through slavery. They also have more of a choice in the matter than Blacks about whether they are willing to affiliate or not. As we pointed out in chapter 2, depending on skin color, accent, or other behavioral choices, many Latinos can choose to pass as White and can escape the claws of racism. The Latino community is experientially, racially, and economically diverse: they come from different countries, have different levels of Spanish-speaking ability, and grew up with different degrees of a Hispanic embrace. While they have many elements of shared communal affinity, they have to work harder at embracing that affinity.

This difference between Blacks and Latinos in the nature, depth, and extent of the shared experience then sets up a different context for a sense of collective power—or powerlessness. Blacks have more of a shared understanding that power dynamics are a major factor affecting their lives; therefore, they tend to have a greater sense of commitment to prioritize the confrontation of this make-it-or-break-it reality.

FAITH AND RELIGION

In the absence of any form of recourse outside the slave system, Blacks turned to the church as a way to survive. The Christianity forced on their slaves by White slave owners was a form deeply distorted to provide a rationale for slavery. The owners believed that converting their slaves to this religion would lead them to accept their fate. Instead, Blacks appropriated the Christianity of their owners and made it their own. They recognized that the Bible was a story of liberation from slavery, that the plantation owner was Pharaoh, and that the Jewish slaves of the Old Testament were the Black slaves of their time. Their leaders, such as Frederick Douglass and Harriet Tubman—and in the post-slavery era, Malcolm X, Dr. Martin Luther King, Jr., and others—were their Moses.

The Black churches helped to solidify spiritual and communal strength within the African-American community. Over the centuries these churches evolved with countless acts of faith and resistance, piety, and protest. The churches were—and remain—sustained and animated by the idea of freedom and liberation. This strength makes it easy to comprehend how Black churches have served as the foundation for organizations such as the Southern Christian Leadership Conference and, of course, the civil rights movement. With the support of their churches, African Americans developed a long history of engaging in peaceful marches and participating in nonviolent movements to demand what they envisioned as just and righteous.

In contrast, the Latino collective psyche is grounded in Catholicism, even for those Latinos who have converted to Protestantism. Devout Catholics often point to the religious vows of poverty, chastity, and obedience. When Spain colonized Latin America, the Catholic church played a key role. Its priests gave sermons on the virtues of being obedient and subservient, having a "God willing" mentality, and accepting one's place in life. White slave owners failed to instill a mind-set of subservience in their Black slaves through Christianity. In contrast, the subjugated populations in Latin America accepted this message of passivity. So it is understandable that Latinos developed less of a willingness to engage in conflict.

EDUCATIONAL, NOT-FOR-PROFIT, AND POLITICAL INSTITUTIONS

As the shackles of slavery were broken, and out of the ferment of Black liberation after the Civil War, the historically Black colleges and universities (HBCUs) emerged. HBCUs such as Spelman College, Howard University, Morehouse College, and 104 more are a source of great pride for the Black community because of the lengthy and significant role they have played in educating young African-American men and women. Some of these schools are over one hundred years old and have long lists of accomplished alumni. The experience of attending an HBCU further solidifies shared communal responsibility and emboldens African Americans to pursue power for the benefit of the greater good.

In contrast, there are the HSIs, which have been designated as such only since 1992. According to the Hispanic Association of Colleges and Universities (HACU), a nonprofit national educational organization, there are 470 HSIs enrolling two-thirds of all Hispanic college students. These institutions have not yet reached the stature of the HBCUs, though during the Obama era they began to strengthen their structural foundations and grow through increased governmental and individual donor contributions. But they are still early in their journey compared to the much more established HBCUs.

In politics, look no further than the Congressional Black Caucus, a much larger and, many would agree, more powerful and vocal group than the Congressional Hispanic Caucus. Also consider the impact of African-American advocacy organizations such as the National Association for the Advancement of Colored People (NAACP), the National Urban League (NUL), and the People United to Serve Humanity (Rainbow PUSH Coalition).

Latinos also have powerful platforms, such as the United Farm Workers (UFW)—with its heyday being the 1970s under César Chávez—the National Council for la Raza (renamed UnidosUS in 2017), the League of United Latin American Citizens (LULAC), the Mexican American Legal Defense and Educational Fund (MALDEF), and similar organizations. But in contrast to the Black organizations, they are not as deeply embedded in the power dynamics of American institutions and government.

The Black institutions and organizations created platforms from which emerged a long list of leaders championing the cause of African-American rights, in addition to those mentioned earlier: Frederick Douglass, W.E.B. Du Bois, Sojourner Truth, Harriet Tubman, Rosa Parks, Malcolm X, Reverend Jesse Jackson, and President Barack Obama. Latinos can proudly point to César Chávez, former San Antonio mayor Henry Cisneros, and Supreme Court Justice Sonia Sotomayor, but their list of household-known names runs much shorter than that of the African-American community.

COMPARING RESPONSES TO POWER

Now we layer in the cultural elements that also have influenced African-American responses to power dynamics. Through our analysis of power and the African-American experience, we've learned that their community has a much more developed understanding of—and appreciation for—what it takes to obtain more influence in corporate settings. Their familiarity with power, gained through a sustained, cohesive, and long history of struggle for equality through conflict, enables them to be more comfortable with the discord and tension brought by that pursuit of power. Most important, they've learned to leverage their shared responsibility as the rationale and the source of strength to engage in the struggle.

The shared responsibility is carried over into the workplace by African-American executives. There they may stand up more boldly on issues that may impact them not just as individuals, but as part of the African-American population. They may say, "I'm not doing this so much for me, but I'm willing to fight this fight for our community." We've learned that this collective responsibility is so prevalent that George Fraser, an accomplished African-American CEO and author of the book *Click: Ten Truths for Building Extraordinary Relationships*, wrote, "African-Americans of means who do not reach down and lift up their own, and are not philanthropic at some level, should be socially isolated and ostracized."[2]

So why were African Americans in the Cobbs and Turnock book so expressive in their views on power, yet our Latino executives more subdued? We surmise that Latino executives seem less willing to invite disturbance, which means they are less willing to joust for position and advantage when it comes to acquiring and wielding power.

Part of this uneasiness with conflict likely comes from the strong Latino cultural trait known as *simpatía*—a general tendency to seek positive relationships with others, which then makes it difficult to engage in personal conflict.

In their 1991 study on Latino behavior, Gerardo Marín and Barbara Vanoss Marín found that because of *simpatía*, Latinos tend to suppress behaviors that are considered forceful or overly aggressive.[3] Similarly, in 2003, author Norma Carr-Ruffino found that Latinos are more likely to avoid aggressive stances on subjects because they want others to think well of them.[4]

Consequently, Latinos often enter corporate America with conflicting thoughts and feelings about obtaining, maintaining, or using power. Non-Latinos often observe that Hispanics are not as successful at chasing power because deep down they think power is objectionable, or even illicit. Thus they develop a proclivity to stand back and respond passively. This lack of aggressiveness in the pursuit of power may partly explain the dearth of Latino executives in the C-suites. George Herrera says:

> I don't think that we fight for power well. We don't unite to pursue power like African Americans do. I think that one of the problems is that Latinos continue to have this feeling of vulnerability, of just feeling scared—and that's unfortunate. We don't have the willingness to go out there and really rattle the cages.

An executive coach who works with many Latino and Black leaders reinforces this point, sharing that his Latino clients are excessively concerned with how they are perceived by others. He cited several examples of Latinos who didn't want to press certain issues because they felt others would consider them too aggressive. On the subject of advocating for Latino causes, the coach described many who didn't want to be perceived as forcefully pushing the Latino agenda. By comparison, his African-American clients are much less worried about how others perceive them or about being considered too aggressive. More important, they feel an obligation to advocate for African-American issues, regardless of what others may think.

Latinos Must Forge Their Own Path to Greater Power

To be clear, we are not saying that style-wise there is a right or wrong way to interact with power. Nor are we saying that Latinos are not capable of engaging in displays of power that involve conflict. We are simply advocating for Latinos to engage in a dual process: being less ambivalent about power, and at the same time mastering an approach to power that is grounded in, but does not conflict with, Latino sensitivities and ethos.

RESOLVING POWER AMBIVALENCE

When, as consultants, we see the need for culture change in our work, rather than proposing the adoption of another group's culture values and preferences, we seek to learn from others' experiences and then look for things within the culture that can actually be tapped to motivate the change.

For example, the values of *familia* (family), *comunidad* (community), and *simpatía* (solidarity/affection) for Latinos are elements that can contribute significantly to creating and nurturing an environment of high involvement—characteristics we don't want to lose. However, as we saw in chapter 4, cultural virtues can also have a shadow side, and in the case of Latinos, even these positive cultural attributes have served to undermine our ability to be as powerful as we can in corporate America and have diminished the collective impact we can offer in the advancement of Latinos into managerial and leadership roles.

What is it within our culture that we can tap into to motivate a behavioral change when it would seem to contradict our deeply cherished notions of how to interact with others? In this case, we believe our appeal must raise awareness that we have fallen short of fully living up to our communal values.

How can this be? One of the big contradictions in Latino culture in the U.S. is that for all our love for *la familia* and our self-image of being a communal people, we are actually allowing our differences within the Latino community to create divisions (as we saw in chapter 3). These divisions are fundamental to our inability to mobilize collective action with a power commensurate to our total numbers.

By failing to fully display our values of *comunidad*, we not only contribute to exclusion in a world rife with people being discriminated against because of their differences, but actually impede our collective ability to advance—and individual Latinos' ability to rise to their full potential. Thus we further lessen the impact Latinos can demonstrate in enhancing the performance of corporations—and the impact we can have on the U.S. society and economy as a whole. Knowing how we hurt ourselves should give us greater *coraje* (courage) to speak truth to power more frequently—not just in a pleading or polite way, but in an assertive and powerful way.

Greater courage is needed—and we have the tools at our disposal to summon it. We possess assets within our own culture to celebrate and to be proud of. These assets are potential sources of greater Latino power. As we leverage them, we can construct a distinctive Latino response to optimizing power.

Latino Cultural Assets as Power Differentiators

What are these cultural assets we can leverage more powerfully? In chapter 4 we outlined various ways corporate America can benefit from Latino culture. Now we offer three cultural assets that Latinos can tap within themselves to become more powerful.

THE POWER OF BIOGRAPHY

In a vastly diverse world posing both threats and opportunities to business, it is not enough to have employees with book knowledge and finely honed skills and competencies. The systemic disruption taking place in every industry requires alternative ways of seeing, interpreting, and devising responses.

Latino biographies, when embraced and understood in all their complexity and richness, can be mined by the individuals themselves to offer a different perspective. Latinos who have worked through their cultural identity are also well positioned to better understand the similar journeys customers and coworkers face as they seek products, services, and meaningful work.

To utilize their backgrounds powerfully, Latinos must consistently engage in cultural reflection and soul searching as it relates to Latino biography. Doing so enables Latino leaders to lead in a centered way from their differentiated biographies to take bolder stands.

And because, as a community, our average age is younger than for most other ethnic/racial groups, our power comes from hope for a better tomorrow and lies in the talent, biography, and possibilities associated with youth.

THE POWER OF A GLOBAL AND BICULTURAL PERSPECTIVE

Latinos are not always bilingual, but they are almost always bicultural. This means they are adept at moving effectively in varied cultural environments and have leveraged this skill to be accepted. But what is the impact when they introduce new cultural values, behaviors, and skills into an environment unaccustomed to diversity? Jorge Figueredo observes:

> My bicultural background absolutely helped me with my career. I was able to recognize not only that

I was different but that there could be various ways of looking at the same thing. That not only gave me greater insight, it also helped me to more effectively recognize that there were multiple points of view that needed to be heard and addressed in any room.

Victor Arias leverages his bicultural identity to be able to transcend many lines that often are kept separate in society:

There's a switch in my head, and I always keep it on. While I spend a lot of time with executives in my board and executive search work, I go out of the way to talk to and connect with the housekeeper at the hotel as well. I also pay attention to how people, including executive candidates, treat other people not like them, and that's a really big filter for me.

When Lou Miramontes was offered an expat assignment in Mexico, he found the situation ironic:

My *abuelita* (grandmother), who lived across the street from me, said, "Why are you going to Mexico? Do you know how hard it was for your grandfather to get here and now you're going back?!" I talked to the chairman about her concern and he told me, "They think you're one of them in Latin America, but we also know you're one of us in the United States. You have to be cross-cultural, multilingual. You have to be able to play in all those buckets." I learned how to be bicultural, resulting in great effect on those around me, on emerging Latino talent, and for my career.

Because ours is a history shaped by twenty-seven different nations, Latinos epitomize what it means to be global. We can provide the ideal archetype to corporate America of what a global leader must be. Ours is a community with a rich history of bringing globally diverse groups together to construct a collective identity, a unique gift offered by Latinos.

THE POWER OF SACRIFICE

Millions of Latinos are in the U.S. because of huge risks their great-grandparents, grandparents, or parents took in uprooting themselves from their homeland to seek a better life in *El Norte* (The North) for their children and their children's children.

For nearly sixty million Latinos, the massive migration has—for the most part—paid off, and now U.S. Latinos are the ninth-largest economy in the world. For us as a people, this ability to do a large-scale relocation and, in that, positively influence another culture and economy means that we have operated with transformational power in the past. We can do so again today by flexing the power of our numbers and love for this country to counteract rising anti-immigrant attitudes and policies.

Juana Bordas said it best in her book *The Power of Latino Leadership*: "Latino power is rooted in history and tradition, an understanding that the past is the rich soil that nourishes tomorrow. Latinos owe a great debt to the leaders who have paved the way for our community to blossom."[5]

Latino power thus dictates that supporting the greater Latino community is not an option, but rather an obligation. Luis Ubiñas states, "Anything less is a dishonor" to those who paved the way. We believe Latinos will continue to advance as a community because we see our ties to others as a series of mutual obligations and privileges connecting us to our past, connecting us now, and connecting us into our shared future. If we teach Latino millennials and Gen Xers to build on the legacy of those who paved the way, our community will continue to more powerfully inject corporate America with the many benefits associated with Hispanic heritage.

Sandra Rivera, chief people officer at Intel Corporation and member of the company's Hispanic Leadership Council, elaborates on the responsibility that Latino executives have to be more successful in giving back to the Latino community, especially when it has served as a foundation for their personal success:

> I realized that all of the ways that I was being successful in my career and all of the contributions that I was making are very much rooted in these Latin heritage values that I grew up with. As I became more aware of that, I started to feel the responsibility to pay it forward and to advocate for the broader Latino community. Because I'm actually the highest-ranking Hispanic leader at Intel now, I feel even more responsibility to make sure that I am supporting Latinos.

This type of sacrifice amplifies Latino power.

The Latino Collective Can Ground Our Relationship to Power

By leveraging our uniquely Latino assets, we can now claim our own approach to power, one that comes from a goal of advancing the collective. We see power stemming from the community for the greater good. Given our proclivity for *simpatía*, our attitude toward power is grounded in our relational approach to leadership.

The Latino approach to power is desperately needed by today's hyperpolarized society. We are well suited to build bridges of understanding and cooperation. We can no longer afford to stand idly by and let others walk over *our* bridges on their own march for more power and influence.

Sandra Rivera describes why Latino executive advocacy is so important:

> Other Latino executives at Intel and I feel we need to create a community of support to identify young Latino leaders we want to nurture, and to make sure we are attracting, retaining, and growing Hispanic talent. We are dedicated to our Latino employee population that might otherwise not be supported. Through our positions of authority, we give them support and the self-confidence they need to achieve greater levels of success.
>
> But that nurturing needs to be a very directed effort. It isn't going to happen by chance. We realized that if we want to have a vibrant Latin community that is contributing to Intel, we have to make a specific effort. Our Latino executive community is really very committed from a leadership perspective to pay it forward, and we must bring our Latino community along. We have a deep level of commitment to provide support, advocacy, and visibility. Because if we are not nurturing our Latino talent, they may never really achieve everything they are capable of.
>
> With great power comes great responsibility, so I do feel that sense of responsibility, especially as a Latina. We take care of our brothers, our sisters, our parents, our grandparents, and our community. That's what we do.

George Herrera takes seriously the responsibility that comes with greater power. He shares a story of an experience when he was CEO of the U.S. Hispanic Chamber of Commerce (USHCC). The situation involved an internal and biased policy at a major corporation that adversely impacted the Latino business community. George took an approach that unequivocally leveraged power. He didn't let the issue go unnoticed and made the corporation aware that he knew of the internal policy. He was willing to address the issue with the senior-most executives at the company, including the CEO and board chair. He didn't let the company off the hook when they offered to simply write a big check for the USHCC. He didn't succumb to peer pressure when other Latinos suggested he should back off. And finally, he conveyed a willingness to expose the unfair practice to the broader community.

The end result was a favorable solution by the company that led to tremendous benefits for Hispanic business owners, as well as to the corporation, which was able to reap the rewards of greater market expansion due to resolving the impasse—all in response to George's power moves.

While George's example showcases that Latinos can also play the power game, we are still left with the cultural ambivalence that many Latinos feel about wielding more power. So how can Latinos move past these mixed feelings about power, in ways that are congruent with our cultural values? We offer the following guidelines:

- Power will come when forged through collaboration, because it leverages our strength in building relationships. Yet we must accept that we won't always maintain *simpatía* with others when we are advocating for the advancement of the Latino talent agenda. We have to learn to accept and live with uncomfortable power dynamics instead of perpetuating our acquiescence.

- We must acknowledge that no one will just *give* us power, so we must always be in the pursuit of it. Furthermore, we must recognize that when we withdraw from the power game, it's not about being nice; rather, it's abdication.

- We must speak truth to those in power (the majority culture) about the corporate 5 percent shame and about how corporations need to put action behind their claims of valuing diversity. Those words are meaningless if executives of the majority are not willing to lead the change. We also need to speak truth to those leaders *within* our Latino community who aren't doing enough and to celebrate those whose actions advance diversity.

- Our concern for the collective good of the Latino community obligates us to challenge injustices imposed on Latinos. Whenever we feel personal unease in advocating for Latino issues, we can gain strength, courage, and resolve by leveraging our existing mind-set wherever the needs of the Latino community supersede any one of our individual needs.

This Latino-grounded approach to power can manifest itself in the workplace in a variety of impactful ways. It can be on display whenever Latino executives sponsor or strongly advocate for other worthy Latinos during talent reviews. We strengthen our communal position whenever the top Hispanics at a company push to establish, for example, an internal Latino officer caucus to advocate for internal Latino talent. The broader Latino community benefits whenever there is robust advocacy for, and participation in, Hispanic nonprofits and professional associations by visible Latinos from the C-suites.

We gain awareness and perspective when there is full-throttle support to bring in external Latino thought leaders, authors, and consultants. We build collective strength when we gather the resources to send young professionals to Latino leadership development programs offered by academia and nonprofits. We win respect when our Latino leaders protest the massive deportations happening under the Trump presidency in the same manner as African-American executives have done in response to the Black Lives Matter movement. And we can all rejoice when every Latino executive has a ready answer when asked, "What have you contributed to the greater Latino collective?"

Y allí está (And there it is.) Ready to seize the day?

CHAPTER 9

The Next Generation of Latino Leaders: Latinx Learns, Challenges, and Rises

Preferiría ser la cola de un león que la cabeza de un ratón.

I would rather be the tail of a lion than the head of a mouse.

—Daddy Yankee (Ramón Luis Ayala Rodríguez)

The personal and professional biographies of the executives we interviewed—with stories of struggle and triumph, lessons learned, new paths forged—generated insights and wisdom that we have sought to capture as a definitive guide to Latino career success.

Given that the boomer Latino executives grew up and then prospered in an earlier time, how relevant are their experiences and their choices for climbing the rungs of the corporate ladder to Latinos one or two generations later—the ones for whom this manifesto is primarily intended?

To find out how much these different generations do or do not have in common when facing and resolving the challenges of assimilation pressures and cultural identity as they sought career success, we conducted further research, comparing the generational experiences to see how many of the lessons learned were transferable. Where do Latino Gen Xers and millennials face the same or different dynamics? How are their responses similar or different? Do they have blind spots where the perspective of the generation before them could open their eyes?

The research included:

- Five separate focus groups consisting of Latino millennials and Gen Xers, to capture regional and family national origin diversity. We conducted one group each in Dallas, New York, and Los Angeles, and two in Chicago. Each group had between five and ten young, upwardly mobile Latino professionals working in corporate America, with a total of thirty-eight participants.

- An online survey of young Latino professionals conducted during August and September 2020. In total, 302 Latino professionals completed the survey, answering questions related to their identity, education, and aspects of Hispanic heritage they found helpful or detrimental to their career success.

- One-on-one interviews with four young Latinos who have been identified as rising stars within their organizations and are actively involved in their community. By exploring more deeply some of their aspirations, experiences, and thoughts on a variety of topics, we wanted to learn what challenges they were facing, and whether they were performing and behaving differently from their predecessors.

- Multiple large group dialogues we have facilitated with up-and-coming Latino talent in a range of corporations and universities.

- Many formal conversations with young Latinos we have mentored, as well as informal conversations in our daily personal and professional lives.

Before we delve into our findings, let's have a look at the demographic realities of younger Latinos.

Youth is a defining characteristic of the nation's Latino population. A review of the 2016 Pew Research Center study, titled "The Nation's Latino Population Is Defined by Its Youth,"[1] reaffirms that Hispanics are the youngest major racial or ethnic group in the U.S. With an average age of twenty-eight, Latino youth are making an important contribution in countering the challenges presented by the aging of the U.S. population, especially when compared to similar economies such as those of China and Japan. With the youngest population among all ethnicities and races in the country, Latinos represent the core of the future of American society.

KEY FINDINGS FROM THE PEW RESEARCH CENTER STUDY, "THE NATION'S LATINO POPULATION IS DEFINED BY ITS YOUTH"

- About one-third of the nation's Hispanic population is younger than eighteen, and about a quarter of all Hispanics are millennials. Altogether, nearly six in ten Hispanics are millennials or younger.
- The median age of Hispanics—twenty-eight—is well below that of the major racial groups. For example, the median age among European Americans is forty-three. For Asians, the median age is thirty-six. For Blacks, the median age is thirty-three.
- Among the nation's millennials, Hispanics constitute a larger fraction (21 percent) than they do of all U.S. adults (15 percent).

- Hispanic millennials are much less likely to be immigrants and are more likely to speak English proficiently than other age cohorts. They are also more likely than older generations to be of Mexican origin.

- Nearly half (47 percent) of U.S.-born Latinos are younger than eighteen. By comparison, just 27 percent of U.S.-born Blacks and 20 percent of U.S.-born European Americans are younger than eighteen.

- The median age among foreign-born Latinos is more than twenty years older than that of U.S.-born Latinos (forty-one and nineteen years, respectively).

This new generation of Latinos is also starting to rebrand themselves as Latinx, so in this chapter we too will begin to make this transition when referring to Latino Gen Xers and millennials (see sidebar for the whys of the rebranding).

What did we find out about Latinx under age forty (as we will categorize them, for purposes of this discussion)? As with every generation they have their own set of assets and liabilities. Among their assets, we discovered that Latinx are:

- Asserting their Latinx-American bicultural identity in the workplace with more confidence than any previous generation

- Approaching their career development and advancement in an organized and sophisticated way

- Being adamant about not receiving advantages just because they are Latinx

- Seeking power more comfortably and explicitly

Among their liabilities, Latinx professionals face some unique challenges and potential blind spots:

- An individualism that can undermine serving the community
- Diminished Spanish-language and Latino culture fluency and knowledge
- Relocation reticence
- Lack of Latino role models

Let's now explore these cultural assets and liabilities in more detail.

Latinx Assets

Woven throughout the pages of this book is a driving assumption that Latino heritage is a trove of cultural riches that must be mined to add value to personal identity, as well as to quality of leadership. But there are generational shifts within ethnic cultures, and Latinx professionals' cultural and generational assets manifest in some distinct ways compared to boomer Latinos.

A BICULTURAL IDENTITY

The most important aspect of the Pew Research Center study was its declaration that Latinx professionals have a strong connection to both their Hispanic and American cultures: "Latino millennials and Generation Xers are bilingual Americans who are assimilated into American society but still value the emotional connection to their Hispanic heritage—they are bicultural."

This finding reinforces our observations from chapter 3 that one of the most powerful ways for Latinos to overcome our intra-Latino divides is to embrace a pan-Latino and American mainstream bicultural identity. Latinx are leading the way in this pursuit, and in this respect their story is not following the total assimilation arc of previous immigrant groups who came to the U.S.

When most immigrants arrive in a new country, they tend to take a relentless linear path toward assimilation. Each successive generation in the new country undergoes a further process of assimilation and dilution of cultural identity. This assimilation usually takes hold across three main components:

- Immigrants tend to adopt English as their primary language.
- Immigrants embrace the American work ethic of being individually self-reliant and benefiting fairly from their hard work.
- Immigrants are expected to take pride in their homogenized American identity.

We learned, in our discussions with Latinx, that many are moving away from the melting pot mythology of straight assimilation into American culture. Though they faced pressures to assimilate, Latinx as a group are choosing to retain their Hispanic identity instead of becoming fully assimilated as would have been predicted based on the trends of earlier immigrants. We were heartened to see that Latinx are not losing their sense of differentiated identity. As one New York focus group participant stated:

> I'm *ambicultural*. I listen to Coldplay and Mark Anthony. I embrace my dual identity.

Seeing it as a worthwhile struggle, Latinx are choosing to fight to maintain their Hispanic identity. Our online survey results indicate that they are so grounded in their sense of identity that an astounding 69 percent of respondents said they have never held back or hidden any part of their Latino ethnicity in the workplace.

In essence, they see their Latino-ness as an asset and differentiator, adopting a bicultural identity in which they still embrace their Americanness. They celebrate and accept their Latino identity as another dimension of who they are. This is not to say that the Latino identity is not a complex issue for Latinx; however, we are saying that Latinx are more unambiguously willing to lean into their identity.

A Latina focus group participant in Los Angeles talked about authenticity and identity, saying:

> The more you hide your Latino background, you become less like yourself. You can be as successful as you want to be; however, when you're not being authentic, are you really successful? That's not really who you are.

We found several reasons for this bicultural acceptance. The sheer size and continued rapid growth of the Hispanic population in the U.S. makes it easier to maintain a connection to Hispanic heritage. Latinx have a plethora of choices if they want to hear Spanish radio, watch Spanish-language TV, hear Spanish music, or eat at Latin restaurants. Because they are surrounded by Hispanic cultural elements, Latinx are finding it easier to maintain the connection to their heritage than did previous generations. A New York focus group participant shared this perspective:

> I arrived in this country back in 2002. Then more people would look at you differently if you had an accent. Now I think there are a lot more Latinos in the United States as a whole. I remember when I first arrived in Missouri, there was like nobody that looked like us, my sisters and me. Now you see Latinos everywhere, even in a place like Missouri.

Latinx see their biculturalism as a competitive advantage in the workplace. Unlike some of our Latino executives who entered organizations at a time when their Hispanic heritage was seen as a disadvantage, today's Latinx are manifesting their biculturalism as part of their career strategy, seeing it as something that will serve them well in business.

Viewing their biculturalism as an asset emboldens them to high-light it in the workplace. A Latina in the Dallas focus group boldly asserted:

> I see my ethnicity as an asset. Being bicultural opens up more doors for me. I am who I am. I have my culture, and it's important to me, *whether people accept it or not.*

In our survey, nearly two-thirds (64 percent) of Latinx felt that the fact they were either bilingual or bicultural was one of the main reasons for their professional success.

WORDS OF WISDOM FROM LATINX LEADERS

José Padilla, *thirty-two, corporate strategy analysis, Netflix*

José is the son of Mexican immigrants. He grew up in the neighborhood of Bell Gardens, just outside East Los Angeles. After earning a bachelor's degree from the University of California, Berkeley, in 2010, he began his career as an auditor at Deloitte. He joined Facebook, Inc., in 2013 and served as the president of Facebook's Latino employee resource group, Latin@, before joining Netflix in 2019. José shared these insights:

Embracing Latino identity at work

I often speak to a lot of Latinos who don't want to embrace their Hispanic heritage because they worry they will be viewed as a token Latino, or others may think they got hired only because of a quota. It's as if identifying as Latino diminishes their cred-ibility and merit. When I have conversations with Latinos who believe that, I advise them that there will eventually come a time when they will be comfortable to say, "Yes, I'm Latino, and this is part of me. I want to bring this part of me to work every day. But I want my own actions and own merits to speak for themselves." And once they do that, they will have more of a willingness and openness to embrace their diversity and leverage it as an asset in the workplace.

On being a role model
Often, when speaking of the lack of diverse leaders in corporate America, people cite that "You can't be who you can't see"—meaning you can't be a leader unless you see people in leadership positions who are Latinos. More and more this inspires me to try to be that leader. Why can't I be the person—the Latino leader—who's at the top and serves as a role model?

On Latino leadership development programs
I have no doubt that Latino leadership programs are necessary and that companies should continue to invest in them. There are a lot of things specific to our Hispanic culture and our ethnicity that affect how we engage in certain situations and in our leadership approach. In fact, I enjoyed helping to put together Facebook's first Latino Leadership Day for all U.S.-based Facebook Latinos at our headquarters a few years ago.

It has been a boost to this phenomenon that for the past twenty years corporate America has amplified its efforts to create more diverse and inclusive work environments, encouraging employees to bring their full selves to work. Many Latinx have accepted this invitation, feeling they can more readily express their biculturalism because corporate America is creating a safe place, or sanctuary, for them. One Dallas group participant told us:

> One of the things that I really like about being bicultural is that it is Latinos who can bridge the

cultures and be mediators to the two sides in the workplace.

By comparison, the Latino boomers who forged a path for them faced more pressure to assimilate. They were surrounded by more prejudice, more resistance, and a general lack of knowledge about Hispanic heritage. Today there is greater emphasis on inclusion, of knowing the difference between right and wrong when it comes to outright discrimination and unconscious bias. All this further confirms that there are benefits to being Hispanic in the workplace. This creates more eagerness and increased motivation for Latinx to say, "Wait a minute. Not only do I not have to hide my Latino identity, but it's actually a good thing to be unapologetic about it. Why not embrace the Latino thing?"

As corporate America creates conditions that nurture biculturalism, with an eye to building their pipelines for future Latino leaders, companies are opening more job opportunities for Latinos who stay connected to their roots; in some cases corporations are actually pressuring these employees to *not* lose their unique voice and biculturalism. Latinx are noticing this demand for Latino talent.

One focus group participant in Los Angeles warned that corporations should continue encouraging young Latinos to be themselves at work, or else the Latinos will leave. She stated:

> My advice to corporations and CEOs is this: Let us be ourselves. Let us be authentic and really tap into that talent. Really nurture our talent, because our talent is who we are; it comes from within. If corporations try to change who we are and change how we see the world, then they're just keeping us in a box where we're not going to be happy. We're not going to excel, to our fullest potential, if you're

trying to change who we are or our values. I'm not going to let anyone change who I am, and I don't care how much money you pay me, I will leave if you won't embrace my talent. I'll walk out that door. I'm always going to stay true to my values, and one of my values is just being authentic and Latino 100 percent of the time.

MILLENNIAL LATINOS INFLUENCING CULTURES WORLDWIDE

The Latinx cultural influence transcends national and racial ethnic lines. Within a mere six months after its release date in 2017, the hit Latin song "Despacito" (Slowly) made history for being the most-streamed track of all time, at 4.6 billion plays globally, according to Universal Music Latin Entertainment.

The song, by Puerto Rican singer Luis Fonsi and reggaeton star Daddy Yankee, and its accompanying remix featuring Justin Bieber, has young Latinos and non-Latinos in the U.S. and around the world singing and dancing.

Recently, Andrés was riding in the car with one of his closest friends, Jason Douglas, who is African American. Jason's teenage son, Mikey, and eight-year-old son, Ethan, were in the backseat. They had all just left a music festival where salsa artist Gilberto Santa Rosa had performed, and Mikey not only danced salsa, but danced it authentically. On the way home, "Despacito" came on, and Ethan was singing along to the Spanish lyrics—not just mouthing the words, but in a way that was clearly internalized. "Despacito" had become his song as well.

Another reason Latinx are embracing their ethnicity unapologetically is that millennials as a group are more open about race and ethnicity. Their greater acceptance of difference makes it easier for Latinx to remain connected to their heritage. A focus group participant in Los Angeles describes the millennial mindset this way:

> While millennials tend to be more judgmental about what your values are and who you are as a person, they are much more open and accepting about other cultures.

SOPHISTICATED CAREER STRATEGY

The older Latino executives we interviewed were ambitious and willing to take risks. In many cases they were pioneers, because they were the first, or the only, Latinos in their environments. They have had career trajectories that are quite impressive. In most cases, however, their careers unfolded as opportunities arose. They followed their instincts and took a somewhat ad hoc approach to their career.

By comparison, our discussions with young Latinx professionals showed they have a clearer outlook, greater maturity, and much more sophisticated approach to their careers. They conveyed a heightened sense of organizational savvy and a more refined career mindfulness. A Latina focus group participant in Los Angeles described her well-thought-out plan for her career:

> When I'm thinking about my career trajectory, I must have a career plan, and I'm calculated about having that plan. I'm always weighing pros and cons, pros and cons, and making sure that each move I make is the right one. But if I fail, that's OK too, as long as I get back on track.

Latinx are also taking a more thoughtful approach to their careers at a much earlier age. Another Los Angeles participant said:

I'm serving on the advisory board of USC, but my long-term goal is to serve on a corporate board. There's so much to do between now and then, but I'm telling people now.

Robert spoke at the University of Chicago for a Hispanic Scholarship Fund Youth Leadership Summit held in July 2019. The summit brought in 150 of arguably some of the brightest high school juniors in the country. They all had well-constructed plans for their future. They knew where they wanted to go, not just for their undergrad degrees but for graduate school as well. Most already knew what type of career they wanted to pursue, and several already had plans to become entrepreneurs. Robert doesn't recall thinking this way when he was a high school junior. This further validates our finding that young Latinos are taking more ownership of their future, and dismissing the *si Dios quiere* (God willing) mentality of earlier generations.

I'M NO VICTIM
While our young Latinx professionals embraced the benefits that come with being bilingual and bicultural, we noticed that they are especially sensitive about programs and initiatives that appear to give them preferential treatment based on their Hispanic heritage. They want to be given opportunities because of the skills and perspectives they bring to the workplace, not because of their ethnic background. A focus group participant in New York told us:

I don't want to be like, "Oh poor little Latina." No. I don't want pity from anyone.

For them, receiving such preferential treatment was the equivalent of others believing that they had the misfortune of being Hispanic, and because of this they needed extra care. Our young Latinos rejected this notion outright.

A Dallas focus group participant described it this way:

> I've always been against minority contracting. I want to compete based on what I do, not where I'm from.

WORDS OF WISDOM FROM LATINX LEADERS

Julissa Ramirez, thirty-three, technical program manager, Google

Julissa was born in the Dominican Republic, the oldest of four, and raised by a single mother. She moved to the Bronx in New York when she was nine and grew up there. She earned bachelor's and master's degrees in engineering, both from the Rochester Institute of Technology. In 2012, she joined Intel, where she led large, global cross-functional programs and projects. She is also a leader in Intel's Latino employee resource group. She left Intel in 2020 to join Google. She shared these insights with us:

On the value of Latino employee resource groups (ERGs)
The Latino ERGs at Intel and Google have given me the opportunity to progress with my Latino self, and I've flourished because of that. I feel more connected to who I am because of those ERG experiences and the opportunities that have been given in the corporate world through the ERG. The ERG also helped me find a community of peers, as well as a professional network and development group that has taken me to heights that I never would have imagined.

On the importance of giving back to the Latino community
To me, giving back to our communities is our duty. The only way we're going to move forward as a community is if we, the ones who have some level of success, go back and reach out

and pull others up. It's the only way. We've got to push up and pull up. This is part of my DNA; I have to do it. I can't really say that I care about my community, and just sit back and do nothing. How will that help the next generation do better?

On her relationship with power
When you said "power," the first word that came to my mind was confidence. "Power" is not a negative word; it means that you have the ability to influence others and that you can effect change. Because I wear my differences on my skin, it can be intimidating to be the only Latina, woman, or person of color in the room. Once you walk in you can do one of two things: you can be affected by it negatively, or you can take the opportunity and show the value you bring to the table because of your differences. I don't see power as an individual thing; I see power as a community/shared thing. Power is not something I can take from someone. I can have my own light, and others can shine just as bright. No one can take the power that I have from me. I see it as something we can build together.

We believe that part of this attitude of rejecting preferential treatment stems from rejection of any notion that being Latino means in some way you are less than someone else. Considering their Latino-ness an asset, Latinx don't feel the need for any added protection or special consideration. One of the Latinas in our Los Angeles group described it this way:

> Rule number one: never play the victim card. That rule is always something that's very key to me.

It's difficult to determine where this strong resentment against handouts and preferential treatment comes from. One theory is that these Latinx professionals grew up with stories about how their grandparents and great-grandparents attended segregated schools, had to drink from different water fountains, or had to flee Cuba to avoid imprisonment. When confronted with these stories, Latinx see examples of triumph and perseverance. Yet they fear that non-Latinos, hearing these stories of discrimination and plight, will feel sorry for Hispanics because of the endured hardships of past generations.

What this means for corporate America is that as programs targeting Latinx become more and more prevalent, they should be positioned to convey the message of leveraging strengths, as opposed to being offered to remedy a perceived deficiency in the Latino community. Instead of positioning such programs as a way to *fix* Latinos or to provide them the tools they *lack*, they should be positioned as efforts to enable Latinos to leverage the strengths that their ethnicity and their unique skills and talents provide.

WILLING TO PLAY THE POWER GAME

The Latinx we spoke to also seemed more willing to embrace power. When asked about their relationship with power, our focus group participants were crystal clear that they passionately pursued power, making these types of comments:

> I want that power, I want that influence, and I rather feel like I'm now seeking that power, or that influence, more than ever before.

> I do seek out power, because I've been at places where the culture is not good. I want to have that level of influence to say, "I determine the culture of this organization, or I determine the culture of this team." Therefore, I'm much more of a power seeker.

> Yes, I compete for power! I really put my name out there where my superiors know that I want to be

recognized as a powerful influence. It feels good knowing that I have that within me.

I'm actively seeking power as part of my long-term plan. I want a seat at the table because I feel like we all deserve to be there.

I want that power, and I've always wanted that power.

When I think about power from a family perspective, I remember growing up with a very family atmosphere where my grandmother was the matriarch; the women were very powerful. Thinking about power in a professional way is not a concept that most women in my family consider. But I would like to change that. I would like power.

These comments reflect a trend that seeking power is a positive attribute. In our online survey, only 17 percent of Latinx felt that having ambivalence toward power had a negative impact on their career. This attitude will serve the Latino community well as younger generations strive to increase Latino influence and impact.

Latinx Liabilities

At times we did notice that young Latinos struggled with aspects of their culture—attitudes that they felt were not positive, that they chose not to embrace. For example, a Latina focus group participant in Chicago shared:

I recall being at home with my mom and my great-aunt while I was in college. My great-aunt offered her opinion, "What's the point of going to school? You just need to get married." I looked at my mom, letting her know I was furious. My mom looked at me and said in a consoling tone, "Just let it be; it's an older way of thinking."

Another focus group participant shared a similar feeling:

I embrace my culture because that's what makes me unique. But there are pieces of my culture that I don't like, like having to dress conservatively, or that women can't leave home until they are married. Those are the pieces that I don't embrace. I'll embrace the food, I'll embrace the celebrations, I'll embrace the things I'm proud of, but the other stuff, I just let it bypass me because it's not part of who I am.

Having heard some state dislikes of their own culture, here are our observations of Latinx liabilities.

INDIVIDUALISM

While we were proud to see that Latinx are more bicultural and are retaining their bicultural identity, we sensed that they have embraced the more European-American values of individualism, displaying a significant focus on personal achievement. We suspect that part of this desire to excel is to repay past generations for the sacrifices they made to provide them with greater opportunities. As mentioned earlier in the book, anything short of success would be a dishonor to those ancestors who paved the way.

However, it was troubling that there was not an equally vibrant stance on leveraging individual achievement to help others. We did not hear many stories about having an obligation to support the broader Latino community. While respondents wished to be connected to the Latino collective and saw their Hispanic heritage as an asset, it seems the communal aspects of Latino culture have been replaced by European-American individualism. In fact, embracing a Latino identity in some ways was seen more as an advantage for *each individual* than as an advantage for the community as a whole.

We hope that as these Latinx professionals mature and accumulate the trappings of individual achievement, they will discover the definition of excellence that encompasses a responsibility to help the larger Latino community to succeed. We are hopeful that Latinx will continue to embrace the vibrant components of their Latin heritage—the salsa, the food, the history, and the culture. Embracing Latino heritage doesn't mean leveraging it simply for personal benefit; doing so also includes having that shared responsibility for the success of the broader Latino community.

LANGUAGE AND CULTURE

An embrace of Latino identity is also connected to Spanish-speaking ability. If Latinx are to be the future stewards of Hispanic heritage in the U.S., they must master the language to better connect with all the richness that being Latino entails. From a practical perspective, being able to read, write, and speak Spanish fluently further enables Latinx to utilize their ethnicity as an asset.

Those who retain their Spanish-speaking ability see being bilingual as an asset in the workplace. A participant in our Dallas group who has his own business outlined the benefit:

> Being bilingual and bicultural helps my business get access to a wider client base, and I'm able to better service the growing Latino market. Many of my competitors can't do that, which benefits me greatly.

Besides connecting to Latino values through language, learning about Latin American culture will serve Latinx well. Studying the history and learning the cultural nuances and national identities of Latin American countries and their people better enables Latinos to gain a more global perspective. This knowledge strengthens bonds within the Latino community and minimizes the ethnic divides that may prevent us from understanding our shared roots.

RELOCATION

Corporations who wish to hire and promote more Latinos often speak of Latinos' general lack of willingness to relocate for career opportunities. We wanted to know how Latinx felt about this perception, and their responses seemed to confirm that moving away from family is still a big issue. This is not surprising when you consider that in our online survey, when participants were asked to describe what aspect of Hispanic heritage had contributed the most to their personal and professional success, 82 percent answered "Family."

Several of our focus group participants mentioned that while they themselves may be willing to relocate, the reaction from their immediate families would be mostly negative. "Why are you leaving us?" "Who is going to take care of us now?" "What are we supposed to do now?" and "You're choosing career over family" were all responses they said they would expect to hear if they told their family they were moving for their work.

Several participants did notice a paradox in that their parents or great-grandparents found the courage to leave their families and home countries to come all the way to the U.S., often with very little money or English-speaking ability. And yet these same family members struggled when their children expressed a desire to move away. A Chicago participant said:

> I like being around my family. That's my culture. What is interesting is that my mom is far away from her family, for they're all still in Mexico. They moved away! They adjusted! Yet they don't want us to move away from them. It's a little bit of hypocrisy.

WORDS OF WISDOM FROM LATINX LEADERS

Jeffrey Martínez, *thirty-seven, executive vice president, PNC Bank*

Jeffrey was born in North Bergen, New Jersey, the son of a Colombian mother and a Cuban exile father. He earned a bachelor's degree from Rutgers in New Jersey. He's a military veteran, having served for nine years in the U.S. Army National Guard, where he did tours of duty in Iraq and Kuwait. After starting his professional career at JPMorgan Chase, Jeffrey joined PNC in 2014. Active in the company's Latino employee resource group, he shared these insights:

On Being Authentic

I remember speaking to Pablo Sanchez, who ran the retail banks for Chase. One of the pieces of advice he offered was this: "Look, I am who I am. And so I align who I am with the companies that find value in who I am." It was probably one of the first times I heard, "Be who you are! There's a company out there who's going to value you."

On Travel as a Means to Connect with Latino Ethnicity

I love to travel, and I've found that it helps to reignite that passion around my heritage. Next week I'll be back in Cuba for the fourth time, and I'd say I've probably been to maybe 70 percent of Latin America. Through travel I experience Latin culture and music. I love seeing it live; being in Argentina, for example, where it's the tango. That has made me proud of my heritage, a passion that was silent when I was a teenager. Whether it's spending time in Lima, Machu Picchu, Colombia, Ecuador, Brazil, Central America, or the Islands, there's something to be really proud of. Today I have no problem going to a tower and screaming out my heritage and my family's story.

On Challenging Ourselves to Give Back
It's tough trying to figure out how to reach a point where we can really give back. We all come from humble means, so we must put our own oxygen mask on first before we can help the other person. As we grow into senior managers and executives, giving back has to be top on our minds, and we must have a strategy for it. But first we must advance to that top spot!

These sentiments raise the probability that Latinos may be more inclined to turn down career opportunities that require relocation. According to our survey results, nearly one-third (30 percent) of participants felt that an unwillingness to relocate has had a negative impact on their career.

Yet we did see that several of our focus group participants realized the importance of relocation, and not just from a career perspective. Some indicated that Latinos need to get out of their safe zone and be ambitious when it comes to relocation. A Los Angeles participant shared:

> I feel like Latinos need to leave California in the sense that they need to open their wings and build their networks. If Latinos are concentrated in just California, we're not going to be able to show people what we can do. If we're not willing to leave California and go work for a company, some other person is. It's important to me that we're open-minded and that we really spread our wings, exploring other cultures and communities. For many of us, California remains a safety net.

Another Los Angeles participant added that a willingness by current leaders to relocate helps even younger Latinos to be more open to relocation. She shared:

> My little brother is my everything, so when I was considering going to New York, I wondered, "If I move, what am I showing?" I wanted him to go to an East Coast university and get that exposure, but if I was not willing to relocate, how can I tell him, "Go experience something else." I thought I'd be hurting him more if I didn't expose my own self to relocation. He could retaliate by saying. "Well, you stayed in California. I want to go to UCLA." I insisted, "No, no, let's try the East Coast. Let's go!"

LACK OF LATINO ROLE MODELS

Our Latinx professionals collectively felt that older, more successful Latinos are not providing much help or mentoring. One reason is that there were very few or no Latinos for them to look up to in their organizations. This idea was expressed by a Dallas focus group participant who said:

> There aren't too many role models or mentors or anyone who can help me get to the next level.

Our survey results confirm this is a real issue in the community: 67 percent of the respondents said that a lack of Latino role models was one of the main hurdles to their career success.

Without role models, Latinos may struggle to advance in their careers and can have difficulty navigating corporate America. Another Dallas participant said:

> I wish I would've had mentors when I was younger, and I wish I had had somebody pushing me harder,

telling me how to do things. Without role models, Latinos have to learn how to climb the corporate ladder the hard way.

Some expressed exasperation with Latinos who had succeeded in the workplace but then failed to help them. Even worse, several shared that successful Latinos were, in fact, making advancement more difficult for the next generation. A Chicago participant expressed exactly this sentiment when he shared:

> My experience has been that as soon as Latinos reach a certain level, they forget about everyone else. And it's weird because if there's a ceiling or roadblock, and they make a crack, they then go back and seal it so everybody else has to struggle to break it again.

In Los Angeles, a Latina participant shared a similar perspective:

> Latinas have probably been their own worst enemy by not wanting to help other Latinas. Even in a Latino organization, that has been my experience.

Unfortunately, we found a similar feeling within our New York focus group as well. One of them told us:

> White sponsors are not threatened because as they're moving up the ranks, they have been more than willing to sponsor me. When Latinos help out, there's a lot of back talk such as this: "I helped you and you should be grateful." As Latinas, we hear that a lot: "Well, you're not grateful for what I did for you." There's a sense of this attitude: "I will do so much for you, but I will not take that hurdle to then sponsor you to the next level."

Our survey data confirms that what these participants described is a reality for many Latinx. Only 13 percent of our respondents said that their most important mentors have been Latino. Even more troubling, our data indicates that Latinx are starting to model the behaviors of Latinos who have made it to the top but then fail to mentor younger Latinos. While Latinx lament the lack of Latino role models and Latino mentors, when asked if they mentor younger Latinx, almost two-thirds (65 percent) indicated they do not!

WORDS OF WISDOM FROM LATINX LEADERS

Patricia Mota, *thirty-five, president,* Hispanic Alliance for Career Enhancement (HACE)

Patricia grew up in East Chicago, Indiana. She is Mexican American and the daughter of hardworking parents. She earned bachelor's and master's degrees from Indiana University. She was recently appointed as a member of the Illinois treasurer's Latino Advisory Council and the Indiana University Latino Alumni Association Board. In 2015, she was named by Negocios Now as one of Chicago's Top 40 Hispanics Under 40. Patricia shared these insights:

On the responsibility of successful Latino professionals
We have to ensure that we are courageous and fearless about achieving our highest potential. We have a huge responsibility to ensure that we're out and visible in our communities, whether it's serving on nonprofit boards, speaking engagements, or volunteering. We must be involved in making decisions when it comes to economics, government, nonprofits, education, and workforce development. We need to make sure that we're aligning what we best bring to the table in

terms of our capabilities and our own strengths to keep the community moving forward.

On what corporations need to do

Companies need to invest more in their Latino employees and make sure that they provide them with holistic programming. One of the biggest areas to become an effective leader, no matter who you are, is to understand yourself and understand what is it that you bring to the table. And part of that is under-standing your culture and your background. A lot of corporations may have their own internal programming or coaching. That's great, but for corporations to accelerate the advance-ment of Latinos within the organization, they need to look for culturally relevant programming.

On how Hispanic heritage impacts her career

It directly translates to what I have the opportunity to do today, which is to lead a national nonprofit organization. We spend a lot of time emphasizing the worth of traditional Latino values. Specifically, being able to connect to the community and learn-ing about young professionals' experiences to connect and help them achieve their highest potential is a priority. A big part of my role is building relationships, and that's important for me in terms of the family values that I grew up with. We must continue to ensure that Latinos are taking care of each other.

LATINOS AND MENTORING

In our surveys, two-thirds of both Latino executives and Latinx professionals indicated that non-Hispanics have been their most important mentors. This finding is not too surprising, given the lower number of Latinos in more senior roles who could serve as influential mentors.

What is surprising, and very concerning, is how much Latino-on-Latino mentoring is occurring. Eighty-nine percent of our Latino executives, who are mostly boomers, indicate that they mentor younger Latinos. But our data suggests that while these Latino execs are actively mentoring, there simply aren't enough of them to mentor the next generation of Latino leaders.

Because a large number of Latinx professionals are not receiving mentoring from Latino leaders, they do not see the value or learn for themselves how to mentor younger Hispanics. This lack of Latino-on-Latino mentoring has a negative impact on Latino career advancement.

The Way Forward for Latinx

Youth have spoken. They are ready to stand on the shoulders of the pioneering Latino and Latina executives who broke new ground and paved the way. But are the entities around them—the government, the schools, the not-for-profits, the corporations—ready to fully capitalize on this rising Latino talent force? We worry that they are not.

In our conclusion that follows, we present what needs to be done to channel the energy, ambition, and vision of Latinx professionals as they seek their rightful place as leaders in their organizations and society. Following the conclusion, we summarize the entirety of our case through our ten-point Latino Executive Manifesto.

Adelante! Forward!

CONCLUSION

Without More Latino Leaders, Companies Will Suffer

*Cuando estas convencido que una causa
es justa, continua luchando.*

When you are convinced a cause is just, keep fighting.

—Rigoberta Menchú, Guatemalan human rights activist
1992 Nobel Peace Prize

We have come to the end of the journey of laying out a guide to Latino career success. We saw that leadership requires education, know-how, and specialized skills. It requires ambition, hard work, risk-taking, and determination. These are, however, universal truths about requirements for leadership in general. This Latino Executive Manifesto also sought out the Latino differentiator. Was there anything unique about the career journeys and the leadership qualities of the twenty executives we interviewed because of their Latino heritage? The answer is an unequivocal yes.

We have seen that for the Latino executives we interviewed, the foundation of their success was their ability and commitment to be *auténtico*. For these Latinos and Latinas, this cultivation of their own good character demanded that they also come to terms with the implications of their Latino heritage. This journey of self-discovery led them to prove the promise of diversity: that having a diverse leadership, management, and talent pool of people with different experiences, backgrounds, and styles provides corporations with a competitive advantage.

We delved into the specifics of how the Latino differential can be revealed in the workplaces and the C-suites of the leaders whose stories we heard. This is not to say that leaders must manifest their Latino identity to be leaders—this has been proven by the many Invisible Latino leaders out there. Our quest was to seek out those leaders who specifically saw their cultural identity as key to being a transformative leader. Hence, our claim that this is a *Latino Executive Manifesto*. For those Latinos who seek executive leadership and at the same time embrace their culture or fear shedding it in their quest to reach the top, the messages in the book have been for you.

After having put the focus on Latinos and what we need to do (that is within our power) to get ahead, we now turn to the outside forces who also have the responsibility, the ability, and the resources to accelerate the advancement of Latino leaders in corporate America. As we brought to light in this book, without more Latinos in the executive ranks, not only will the Latino community suffer; so too will corporations if they don't reflect, at all organizational levels, a nation whose population will consist of more than one-quarter Latinos by 2060.

The best practices to accomplish Latino leadership goals are well known and have been well documented. Here are five actions that government, universities, not-for-profits, and corporations each must do to truly contribute to the rise of a meaningful number of Latino leaders.

What Government Needs to Do

1. Resolve the status of undocumented young people who grew up in the U.S., and put them on the path to citizenship.
2. Create parity in the funding of HSIs. Currently HSIs are underfunded to the tune of 66 cents for every federal dollar per student going to the rest of higher education annually.
3. Prepare to be held accountable by voters for their hostility to education in communities of color.
4. Diversify government leadership and pipeline ranks with Latinos from the emerging talent pool.
5. Publicly challenge corporations to increase their Latino talent pipelines and Latinos in leadership, and withhold contracts unless certain goals are met.

What Universities Need to Do

1. Help Latino parents who did not graduate from college to understand the value of a university degree, and in the process help them access and navigate the many financial and advisory resources available.
2. Aggressively source and attract Latino faculty and administrators to better attract Latino students.
3. Hold faculty and administrators accountable for the graduation rates of Latino students. Too many Latino students make it into college, only to drop out at disproportionately higher rates.
4. Develop an endowment, with contributions not only from traditional donors but also from the Latino community, to help finance the education of Latino students.
5. Include in the core curriculum more content on Latino history, societal contributions, and cultural influences.

What Not-for-Profits Need to Do

1. Prioritize helping Latino students learn how to navigate the college application process and college life socialization.

2. Partner with government and corporations to provide meaningful forward-looking internships providing real-life work experience, each matched with a mentor.

3. Change the mind-set from one that it's a zero-sum game of competing for slices of the funding pie to one in which the collective pie grows exponentially larger through collaboration.

4. Hold their corporate sponsors accountable when they fall short in advancing Latino talent.

5. Be exceptionally clear to corporations about their most unique and effective impact on Latino talent development, and be ready to refer requests that don't match this sweet spot to other Latino not-for-profits.

What Corporations Need to Do

1. Become knowledgeable of Latino culture and values, and stop pressing Latinos to assimilate; instead, create conditions that nurture Latino professional success. Incorporate some Latino culture into their corporate culture, and stop trying to "fix" Latinos.

2. Aggressively accelerate Latino leadership development holistically through internal and/or external leadership development programs, mentorship, and sponsorship, but most important, through pilot stretch assignments.

3. Differentiate among the various Latino talent pools and segmented markets in ways that are as rigorous and sophisticated as marketing campaigns. There is no single Latino talent force in the same way there is no single Latino market.

4. Encourage their highest-ranking Latino leaders and executives to work together to advance the Latino talent agenda through a Latino officer caucus or round table.

5. Provide opportunities for Latinos to influence major corporate and commercial strategic initiatives.

INTEL CASE STUDY: CORPORATE LATINO TALENT BEST PRACTICE

Every January, global technology companies gather in Las Vegas to attend the Consumer Electronics Show (CES) to showcase their latest innovations and technology related to consumer electronics. In 2015, Intel Corporation CEO Bryan Krzanich chose CES to not only highlight Intel's technology advancements; he announced the company's investment of $300 million to increase diversity in its workforce. As of this writing, it was the largest diversity investment by a technology company, and it supported a pledge that by the year 2020, Intel's U.S. workforce would mirror the talent available in the country.

While the $300 million investment caught the attention of many corporations, it is Intel's long history of successful internal Hispanic initiatives that has long been admired and applauded by the Latino community and has served as best practices for other companies to emulate regarding world-class Latino initiatives.

Intel's top six Hispanic initiatives include:

1. The Hispanic Initiative Program (HIP). Formed in 2006, HIP provides development and retention programs targeting Intel's current Hispanic employees and forges partnerships that position Intel as an employer of choice in the Hispanic community. Under this initiative, Intel offers leadership training, skills development, and networking opportunities to build enthusiasm among Intel's Hispanic employees.

2. Intel Latino Network (ILN). ILN is a chartered strategic employee resource group with chapters located at Intel's U.S. sites. Though ILN's membership is inclusive, their charter is to provide leadership, professional development, and networking opportunities to members and help Latinos advance their careers. ILN is called upon to help in the recruitment, development, and retention of Latinos.

3. Hispanic 1st Year TouchPoint Program. Connects Hispanic employees in their first year at Intel with more experienced peers. The program facilitates integration for recent hires by providing them with resources and assisting them with the creation of their Intel network. When first launched, this program immediately contributed to reducing turnover among first-year Hispanics.

4. Intel Hispanic Leadership Council (IHLC). Dedicated to the advocacy and sponsorship of Hispanics at Intel. Members of the IHLC are the company's most senior Hispanic leaders. They serve as role models of leadership and champions of the company's Hispanic employees, Hispanic talent, and leadership pipeline initiatives.

5. Blueprint for Extraordinary Performance. An internal leadership development series created to address the challenges of isolation, this program leverages a cohort learning model. Latino participants develop tools and skills needed to effectively navigate their careers at Intel, connect with each other, build more effective relationships with their managers and peers, and drive their own development. The program, which ran from 2009 through 2015, ended up with over one thousand alumni.

6. Hispanic Inspire Conference. Its purpose is to strengthen leadership and business acumen. Featuring executive speakers, workshops, and networking sessions, the conference connects employees to important development content and a network of influential peers.

These programs do indeed make a difference. Hispanics who have participated in these various programs and initiatives are retained—and are receiving promotions—at a higher rate than nonparticipants.

HACE CASE STUDY: NOT-FOR-PROFIT
LATINO TALENT BEST PRACTICE

One way companies can increase the number of Latino leaders is to have them participate in Latino leadership development programs offered by not-for-profits.

To uncover the key elements of a successful program, we conducted a focus group of seven Latinas who had completed the Mujeres de HACE (Women of HACE) Leadership Program. The program is run by the Hispanic Alliance for Career Enhancement (HACE) and consists of Latinas participating as a cohort through seven modules delivered over a three-month period.

Through the women's stories of what they had gained from the program, we identified four key beneficial outcomes that helped these women further advance in their careers:

Increased conviction to demonstrate personal resilience to face the challenges of being a leader
By discussing real-life issues, the program helped participants identify triggers, ways of coping, and more productive ways of thinking, feeling, and behaving to maximize their effectiveness.

Sample quotes:

> *I no longer feel intimidated when I'm the only woman or minority leader in the room.*

> *I'm better able to leverage my talents to move up within my company. Not just lateral moves, but moving up to senior roles.*

Deeper connection to the Latino community

Participants developed deep friendships and family-like bonds through the in-depth conversations and shared experiences. Each participant felt she was a teacher *and* a learner during the program. Sample quotes:

Without more Latino leaders, companies will suffer

Sample quotes:

> *I now have this incredible network of people I can reach out to for support and guidance. The network is tremendous.*

> *It's incredible to connect with Latinas who have experienced similar struggles.*

> *I've built bonds and relationships that I will hold forever. I don't feel isolated as a Hispanic any longer.*

Increased confidence

Participants felt better prepared to overcome personal barriers and obstacles that may have diminished their faith in their ability in the past. Sample quotes:

> *Because I'm much more confident, I applied for a job I never would have applied to before.*

> *I've been promoted twice since I completed this program, and now I want to be a vice president someday. I didn't have that aspiration before.*

Greater clarity of their Hispanic heritage

By looking at issues and behaviors through a cultural lens, participants were able to look at their own cultural identity challenges from the perspective of their Latina-ness being an asset rather than a liability. They felt better prepared to join more senior level ranks within their company, while remaining authentic to their Hispanic heritage. Sample quotes:

Now I feel better prepared to become a leader while I'm still being myself and being a Latina.

Since I was born in Latin America, the program has helped me better understand U.S. culture and how my heritage can serve as an asset.

The program is definitely making an impact. Forty percent of participants report a promotion or salary increase within six months of completing the program.

The Legacy of Today's Latino Executives

Llegamos! We got to the end of this book. But this book journey was intended to be just the start of a new era. Building on the legacy of the Latino and Latina executives of a previous generation, as exemplified by the twenty executives we interviewed for the book, it's time to address Latino leadership advancement in a new and disruptive way. One that engages identity rather than buries it, that is authentic rather than imposed; one that treats women and men fully as equals; one that seeks out Latino cultural influences to integrate into the fabric of organizations; and one that looks to the new generation of Latinx to change how we view work, society, and the world.

Latinx—les toca. Latinx—it's your turn.

"*Merece lo que sueñas.*"

Deserve what you dream.

—Octavio Paz

THE LATINO
EXECUTIVE MANIFESTO

INDIVIDUAL

1.

Latino leaders must engage with
and resolve their own cultural identity.

Conclusions will vary for each leader about what it means for them, so we must allow for variances. But it can't be ignored, and the sooner it can be addressed, the more effective Latino leaders will be.

2.

Latinos must embrace ambition
as an honorable intent.

While maintaining humility, we also must not be naïve. No one is going to hand us opportunities if we are not openly seeking them. The community should celebrate those who demonstrate ambition, because we all benefit.

3.

Latinos need to get over our ambivalence about power by claiming more of it and redefining it on our own terms.

Where ambition is personal, power is collective. The impact of Latino power in corporations, government, and society is incongruent with our massive numbers. Yet even as we operate with more power, we must contribute a differentiated way of wielding it.

4.

The next generation of Latino leaders can be more powerful by pursuing the path of a bicultural identity.

Resist assimilation. Instead, develop a differentiating American-Latino identity that embraces and celebrates both the multiple influences of mainstream American culture and that of one's specific Latino heritage(s).

5.

Master the rules of corporate culture so you can break them when the right time comes.

Master the rules of your own culture as well and, in the crucible of being a successful Latino in corporate America, find ways that both cultures can shape and influence each other. In this, create the conditions for greater creativity, innovation, and transformation.

COMMUNITY

6.

Latino leaders must give back to the community.

True excellence requires leveraging high
personal achievement to help others achieve success.
The journey of the Latino executive is incomplete if
they don't give back to others.

7.

Latinos must reclaim our communal spirit to overcome intra-Latino divides.

Focusing on our national, socioeconomic, and regional
rivalries leads to a lack of unity and weakens the power of
our numbers, our institutions, and our leadership.

8.

Latinos need to double down on the relentless pursuit of higher education and rally behind it as a civil rights issue.

Latino college attendance is trending upward, and we
need to accelerate this trend significantly by any means
necessary in the face of massive budget cutbacks.
Education is the greatest bulwark against hostility and
biases, and for achieving the highest levels of leadership.

CORPORATE

9.

Corporations need to
become true meritocracies.

They must shed the self-image that they are unbiased and color-blind, and instead proactively address the conscious and unconscious biases that have kept Latinos from rising to the height of our potential.

10.

Corporations must be willing to adapt
to and capitalize on the differences that
Latinos bring to corporate culture.

Embracing Latino culture will create more inclusive environments for Latino talent and equip companies to better serve Latino consumers and clients. Non-Latinos will benefit from Latino cultural assets in the same way Latinos have been enriched by other cultures.

AN INVITATION

We want to hear from you. Go to www.thelatinxinstitute.com and share with us and the community what the Latino Executive Manifesto means to you. What challenges you the most? Excites you? Makes you think?

Comment on it. Refine it. Share it. Print it. Post it.

We are a rising power in corporate America. Be authentic, be ambitious, be excellent! The Latino community, the broader society, and the corporations you currently serve—or will serve in the future—need more authentic and successful Latino leaders so they can survive and thrive in the twenty-first century.

Now go back into the public square and manifest yourself as a Latino executive.

Latino Executive Manifesto Leaders

Victor Arias, Jr.
Managing Director, Diversified Search
Former Board Member, Popeye's Louisiana Kitchen
Chairman of the Board, Latino Business Action Network

José Armario
CEO, Bojangles' Restaurants Inc.
Board Director, USG Corporation and Avon Products, Inc.

Gilbert Casellas
Chairman, Pine Place Capital
Board Director, Prudential Financial

Patricia Diaz Dennis
Former Senior Vice President, AT&T
Board Member, Entravision Communications Corporation
    and U.S. Steel

The Honorable Cari Dominguez
Principal, Dominguez & Associates
Board Member, ManpowerGroup Inc., Triple-S Management
    Corporation, and The Calvert Funds

Jorge Figueredo
Executive VP, Human Resource (retired), McKesson Corporation

Juan Galarraga
Senior Vice President, Retail Operations, Five Below

Charles P. Garcia
CEO, Tendrel
Former CEO, Sterling Group of Companies
Former Board Director, Winn Dixie Stores (Fortune 500)
Board Member, Junior Achievement USA and Girl Scouts USA

Yvonne Garcia
Chief of Staff to the Chairman and CEO, State
    Street Corporation

George Herrera
Former President and CEO, U.S. Hispanic Chamber
    of Commerce
Board of Directors, Wyndham Destinations

Grace Lieblein
Vice President Global Quality (retired), General Motors
Board Director, Honeywell, Southwest Airlines,
    and American Tower

Monica C. Lozano
President and CEO, College Futures Foundation
Former Chairman and CEO, U.S. Hispanic Media, Inc.

Louis (Lou) P. Miramontes
Senior Partner (retired), KPMG
Board Member, Rite Aid Corporation, Lithia Motors Inc.,
    and OPORTUN Financial

Luis (Lou) P. Nieto, Jr.
President, Nieto Advisory, LLC
President (retired), ConAgra Consumer Foods

Lisa Garcia Quiroz
Former President, Time Warner Foundation
Senior Vice President, Chief Diversity Officer, Time Warner, Inc.

Paul Raines
Former CEO, GameStop Corporation
Former Board Member, J. C. Penney Company

Darren Rebelez
President and CEO, Casey's General Stores
Board Member, Global Life and Casey's General Stores

Sandra Rivera
Executive Vice President and Chief People Officer,
    Intel Corporation

Myrna Soto
Chief Strategy and Trust Officer, Forcepoint
Board Member, CMS Energy, Consumers Energy,
    Spirit Airlines, and Popular Inc.

Luis Ubiñas
Board Member, Electronic Arts, Tanger Outlets, Boston Private
    Financial Holdings, EBSCO Industries, and Mercer Funds

Survey Results

We conducted two separate online surveys to capture the beliefs, sentiments, and experiences of Latino executives and Latinx professionals. The Latino Executive Survey was fielded between March and April 2017 and received twenty responses. The Latinx Professional Survey was fielded between April and May 2017 and received 302 responses. Here are some of the most interesting answers. Specific findings from the overall results have been used throughout the book to support various observations.

Where were you born?

Executives

Gen X/millennials

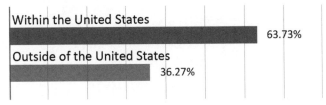

Where were you mostly raised?

Executives

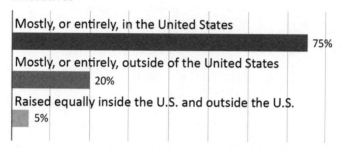

Gen X/millennials

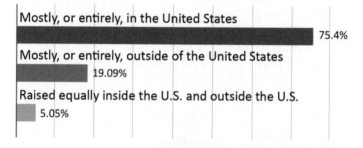

From a language speaking perspective, are you ...

Executives

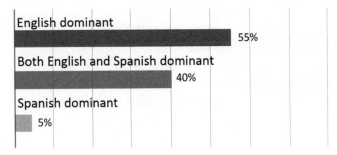

Gen X/millennials

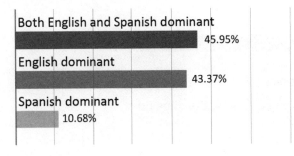

Was Spanish your first language?

Executives

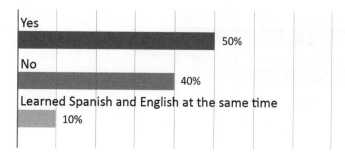

Gen X/millennials

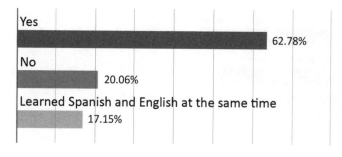

Please identify the five most positive aspects of Hispanic heritage that have contributed to your personal and career success:

Executives

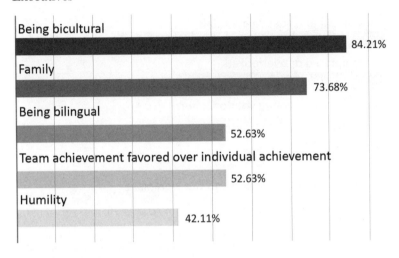

Gen X/millennials

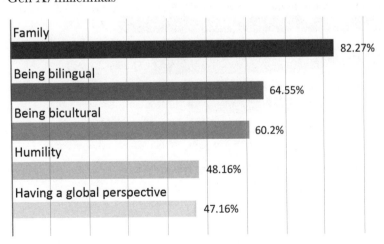

Please identify the five biggest hurdles, as experienced in the workplace, of your Hispanic heritage that have negatively impacted your career:

Executives

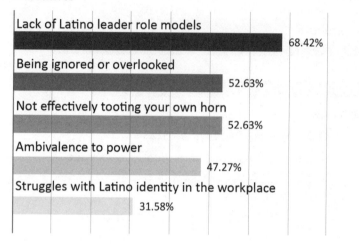

Lack of Latino leader role models — 68.42%

Being ignored or overlooked — 52.63%

Not effectively tooting your own horn — 52.63%

Ambivalence to power — 47.27%

Struggles with Latino identity in the workplace — 31.58%

Gen X/millennials

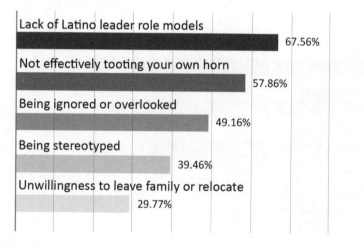

Lack of Latino leader role models — 67.56%

Not effectively tooting your own horn — 57.86%

Being ignored or overlooked — 49.16%

Being stereotyped — 39.46%

Unwillingness to leave family or relocate — 29.77%

Regarding your Latino heritage, how much have you chosen to show in the workplace?

Executives

I have not held back or hidden any part of my Latino identity
57.89%

I have had to hide or downplay some parts of my Latino identity
31.58%

I identify as Latino in my personal life, but not in the workplace
5.26%

I don't identify as Latino in my personal life or in the workplace
0%

Gen X/millennials

I have not held back or hidden any part of my Latino identity
69.26%

I have had to hide or downplay some parts of my Latino identity
22.64%

I identify as Latino in my personal life, but not in the workplace
4.05%

I don't identify as Latino in my personal life or in the workplace
1.01%

In the settings when you were in the minority in the workplace, how did it make you feel? (Check all that apply.)

Executives

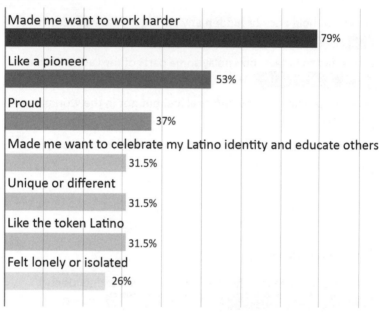

Gen X/millennials

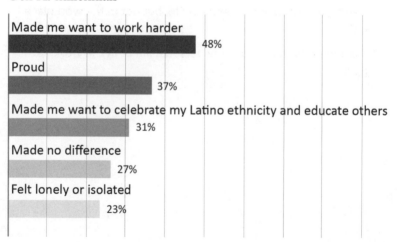

In addition to having the right skills and achieving results, what do you consider the top five keys to your career success? Rank order the top five:

Executives

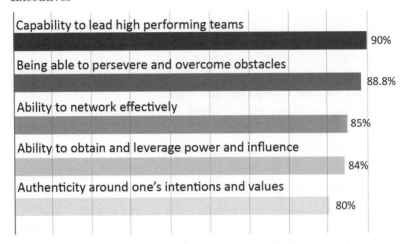

Gen X/millennials

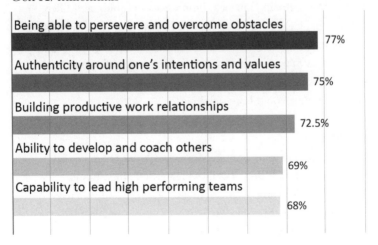

NOTES

Why a Second Edition of Auténtico?

1. Centers for Disease Control and Prevention, "Covid-19 Hospitalizations and Deaths by Race/Ethnicity" (continuously updated), https://www.cdc.gov/coronavirus/2019-ncov/covid-data/investigations-discovery/hospitalization-death-by-race-ethnicity.html.

2. U.S. Bureau of Labor Statistics, "Employment Status of the Hispanic or Latino Population by Sex and Age," in *Current Population Survey*, https://www.bls.gov/news.release/empsit.t03.htm (accessed September 4, 2020), Tables A and A-3.

3. Paul Ong, "Systemic Racial Inequality and the Covid-19 Renter Crisis," UCLA Center for Neighborhood Knowledge (August 2020).

4. Emma Dorn, Bryan Hancock, Jimmy Sarakatsannis, and Ellen Viruleg, in "COVID-19 and Student Learning in the United States: The Hurt Could Last a Lifetime," McKinsey and Company (June 1, 2020), https://www.mckinsey.com/industries/public-and-social-sector/our-insights/covid-19-and-student-learning-in-the-united-states-the-hurt-could-last-a-lifetime#.

Reader Note

1. Luis Noe-Bustamante, Lauren Mora, and Mark Hugo Lopez, "About One-in-Four U.S. Hispanics Have Heard of Latinx, But Just 3% Use It," Pew Research Center (August 11, 2020), https://www.pewresearch.org/hispanic/2020/08/11/about-one-in-four-u-s-hispanics-have-heard-of-latinx-but-just-3-use-it/.

Introduction

1. Price M. Cobbs and Judith L. Turnock, *Cracking the Corporate Code: The Revealing Success Stories of 32 African-American Executives* (New York: AMACOM, 2003).

2. Kevin Cashman, *Leadership from the Inside Out: Becoming a Leader for Life* (San Francisco, CA: Berrett-Koehler, 2008).

3. Richard Fry and Paul Taylor, "Hispanic High School Graduates Pass Whites in Rate of College Enrollment," Pew Research Center's Hispanic Trends Project (May 09, 2013), http://www.pewhispanic .org/2013/05/09/hispanic- high-school-graduates-pass-whites-in -rate-of-college-enrollment/.

4. Tessa Berenson, "How Latinos Drive America's Economic Growth," Time.com (September 15, 2016), http://time.com/4494780/ how-latinos-drive-americas-economic-growth/.

5. Jens Manuel Krogstad, Mark Hugo Lopez, Gustavo López, Jeffrey S. Passel, and Eileen Patten, "Millennials Make Up Almost Half of Latino Eligible Voters in 2016," Pew Research Center's Hispanic Trends Project (January 19, 2016), http://www.pewhispanic.org/ 2016/01/19/millennials-make-up-almost-half-of-latino-eligible -voters-in-2016/.

6. Andrés T. Tapia, "Ya! The Time Has Come for Latinos to Claim Our Place in American Society," *Latin Post* (September 15, 2014), https:// www.latinpost.com/articles/21389/20140915/ya-time-come-latinos -claim-place-american-society.htm.

Chapter 1

1. Michael Hyter and Judith L. Turnock, *The Power of Inclusion: Unlock the Potential and Productivity of Your Workforce* (Ontario: Wiley, 2006).

2. Melinda Wenner Moyer, "Undocumented Immigrants Are Half as Likely to Be Arrested for Violent Crimes as U.S.-Born Citizens," *Scientific American*, December 7, 2020, https://www.scientificamerican .com/article/undocumented-immigrants-are-half-as-likely-to-be -arrested-for-violent-crimes-as-u-s-born-citizens/.

3. Edgar Vargas, Melina Juárez, and Gabriel Sanchez, "Fear by Association: Perceptions of Anti-Immigrant Policy and Health Outcomes," *Journal of Health Politics, Policy and Law* 42, no. 3 (2017): 459–483.

Chapter 2

1. Bernardo Ferdman and Plácida I. Gallegos, "Racial Identity Development and Latinos in the United States," in *New Perspectives on Racial Identity and Development*, ed. C. Wijeyesinghe and B. Jackson (New York: New York University Press, 2001), 32–66.

Chapter 3

1. Ferdman and Gallegos, "Racial Identity Development."
2. Ilan Stavans, *The Hispanic Condition: The Power of a People* (New York: Rayo, 2001).
3. "Mapping the 2012 Latino Electorate," Pew Research Center's Hispanic Trends Project (September 30, 2012), accessed July 29, 2017, http://www.pewhispanic. org/2012/10/01/mapping -the-2012-latino-electorate/.

Chapter 4

1. "Geert Hofstede," The Hofstede Centre, accessed August 03, 2017, https://geerthofstede.com/.
2. Fons Trompenaars and Charles Hampden-Turner, *Riding the Waves of Culture: Understanding Diversity in Global Business*, 2nd ed. (New York: McGraw-Hill, 1998).
3. "Survey Brief: Generational Differences," Pew Hispanic Center (March 2004), http://assets.pewresearch.org/wp-content/uploads/ sites/7/2011/10/13.pdf.

Chapter 5

1. Jens Manuel Krogstad, "5 Facts about Latinos and Education," Pew Research Center (July 28, 2016), accessed July 13, 2017, http://www .pewresearch.org/fact-tank/2016/07/28/5-facts-about-latinos-and -education/.

2. "1986–2011: 25 Years of Championing Hispanic Higher Education," HACU.net (2011), http://www.hacu.net/images/hacu/about/HACU_History_1986-2011F.pdf.

3. Dawn Rhodes, "Northeastern Illinois University to Cut About 180 Jobs: The Devastation Increases," Chicagotribune.com (May 31, 2017), accessed July 13, 2017, http://www.chicagotribune.com/news/local/breaking/ct-northeastern-illinois- university-budget-problems-20170530-story.html.

4. Renee Stepler, "Hispanic, Black Parents See College Degree as Key for Children's Success," Pew Research Center (February 24, 2016), accessed August 05, 2017, http://www.pewresearch.org/fact-tank/2016/02/24/hispanic-black-parents-see-college-degree-as-key-for-childrens-success/.

5. Joseph Hooley, "State Street's CEO on Creating Employment for At-Risk Youths," *Harvard Business Review* (April 26, 2017), accessed August 05, 2017, https://hbr. org/2017/05/state-streets-ceo-on-creating-employment-for-at-risk-youths.

Chapter 6

1. Keith R. Wyche and Sonia Alleyne, *Good Is Not Enough: And Other Unwritten Rules for Minority Professionals* (New York: Portfolio, 2009).

Chapter 8

1. Cobbs and Turnock, *Cracking the Corporate Code*.

2. George C. Fraser, *Click: Ten Truths for Building Extraordinary Relationships* (New York: McGraw-Hill, 2009).

3. Gerardo Marín and Barbara Vanoss Marín, *Research with Hispanic Populations*, Applied Social Research Methods Series 23 (Thousand Oaks, CA: Sage Publications, 1991).

4. Norma Carr-Ruffino, *Managing Diversity: People Skills for a Multicultural Workplace*, 6th ed. (Boston, MA: Pearson Publishing, 2003).

5. Juana Bordas, *The Power of Latino Leadership: 10 Principles of Inclusion, Community, and Contribution* (San Francisco, CA: Berrett-Koehler, 2013).

Chapter 9

1. Eileen Patten, "The Nation's Latino Population Is Defined by Its Youth," Pew Research Center's Hispanic Trends Project, Pew Hispanic (April 20, 2016), www.pewhispanic.org/2016/04/20/the-nations-latino-population-is-defined-by-its-youth/.

BIBLIOGRAPHY

Alvarez, Julia. *How the Garcia Girls Lost Their Accents*. Chapel Hill, NC: Algonquin Books of Chapel Hill, 2010.

Benitez, Cristina, and Marlene González. *Latinization and the Latino Leader*. Ithaca, NY: Paramount Publishing, 2011.

Bordas, Juana. *Salsa, Soul, and Spirit: Leadership for a Multicultural Age*. 2nd ed. San Francisco, CA: Berrett-Koehler, 2012.

Bordas, Juana. *The Power of Latino Leadership: 10 Principles of Inclusion, Community, and Contribution*. San Francisco, CA: Berrett-Koehler, 2013.

Carbajal, Frank, and Humberto Medina. *Building the Latino Future: Success Stories for the Next Generation*. Hoboken, NJ: Wiley, 2008.

Carr-Ruffino, Norma. *Managing Diversity: People Skills for a Multicultural Workplace*. 6th ed. Boston, MA: Pearson Publishing, 2003.

Cashman, Kevin. *Leadership from the Inside Out: Becoming a Leader for Life*. San Francisco, CA: Berrett-Koehler, 2008.

Chong, Nilda, and Francia Baez. *Latino Culture: A Dynamic Force in the Changing American Workplace*. Yarmouth, ME: Intercultural Press, 2005.

Cobbs, Price M., and Judith L. Turnock. *Cracking the Corporate Code: The Revealing Success Stories of 32 African-American Executives*. New York: AMACOM, 2003.

Dabbah, Mariela, and Arturo Poire. *The Latino Advantage in the Workplace: Use Who You Are to Get to Where You Want to Be*. Clearwater, FL: Sphinx Publishing, 2006.

Davidds, Yasmin. *Take Back Your Power: How to Reclaim It, Keep It, and Use It to Get What You Deserve*. Los Angeles: Atria Books, 2006.

Diaz, Junot. *The Brief Wondrous Life of Oscar Wao*. New York: Riverhead, 2008.

Fraser, George C. *Click: Ten Truths for Building Extraordinary Relationships*. New York: McGraw-Hill, 2009.

Gladwell, Malcolm. *Blink: The Power of Thinking Without Thinking*. New York: Back Bay Books, 2013.

Gladwell, Malcolm. *The Tipping Point: How Little Things Can Make a Big Difference*. London: Abacus, 2000.

Hyter, Michael, and Judith L. Turnock *The Power of Inclusion: Unlock the Potential and Productivity of Your Workforce*. Toronto: Wiley, 2006.

Marín, Gerardo, and Barbara Vanoss Marín. *Research with Hispanic Populations*. Applied Social Research Methods Series. 23. Thousand Oaks, CA: Sage Publications, 1991.

Márquez, Gabriel Garcia. *One Hundred Years of Solitude*. New York: Alfred A. Knopf, 1995.

Rodriguez, Richard. *Days of Obligation: An Argument with My Mexican Father*. New York: Penguin, 1995.

Rodriguez, Robert. *Latino Talent: Effective Strategies to Recruit, Retain, and Develop Hispanic Professionals*. Hoboken, NJ: Wiley, 2008.

Stavans, Ilan. *The Hispanic Condition: The Power of a People*. New York: Rayo, 2001.

Tapia, Andrés T. *The Inclusion Paradox: The Obama Era and the Transformation of Global Diversity*. 3rd ed. Los Angeles: Korn Ferry Institute, 2016.

Trompenaars, Fons, and Charles Hampden-Turner. *Riding the Waves of Culture: Understanding Diversity in Global Business*. New York: McGraw-Hill, 2012.

Wyche, Keith R., and Sonia Alleyne. *Good Is Not Enough: And Other Unwritten Rules for Minority Professionals*. New York: Portfolio, 2009.

ACKNOWLEDGMENTS

¡Muchas Gracias!

The two authors are in deep appreciation of:

Henry Cisneros, we have greatly admired your career and are grateful for your continued advocacy for the Latino American community. Your distinguished career is an example of what is possible when one has a guiding purpose and lives by a core set of values. You continue to be an inspiration for the next generation of Latino leaders, and we are humbled that you accepted our invitation to write the foreword for this second edition of *Auténtico*.

Price Cobbs, whose book *Cracking the Corporate Code: The Revealing Success Stories of 32 African-American Executives* was the inspiration for writing this book about successful Latino executives. In his last year of life, he gave us his blessing and his wisdom to follow in his footsteps as well as graced the first edition of this book with the foreword.

Jorge Ferraez and **Pedro Guerrero**—we thank you both for being publishers of two of the most influential publications related to top Latino talent—*Latino Leaders* magazine and *Hispanic Executive* magazine. We are grateful for your insights on our book project, for helping with the focus groups, and for your friendship. We look forward to partnering with you both for years to come as we build the pipeline of future Latino executives.

Jaclyn Tumberger, Pedro's executive assistant at *Hispanic Executive* magazine, you helped us so much with all you did: directions, signage, parking, water, pens, and your overall gracious, helpful, and pleasant self.

Sofía Suarez, thank you for helping us source so many of just the right literary and historical quotes that now open the book and each chapter. This was work that required someone as erudite, well read, and insightful as you. And, of course, we were always grateful for the cocktails and appetizers that greeted us at the end of various working sessions.

A big thank-you to the **Consortium of Latino Employee Organizations** (CLEO) in Chicago. Your active involvement in the Chicago focus groups was extremely valuable. Plus, your participation in our professional survey provided tremendous insights. Keep advocating for Latino professional advancement.

We also want to thank the various people who helped make the first edition possible where their work lives on in this second edition:

Melissa Wilson Giovagnoli, book publishing and social media maven; **Michael Nolan**, our editor; **Kathy Meis**, the publisher; **Joy Dean Lee**, the copy editor and indexer; **Rafael Olivas**, the cover concept designer; and **Gretchen Dykstra**, the proofreader. We are grateful to each of you for the professionalism and high caliber of your work.

Andrés wants to also give **gracias** *to:*
My friend, collaborator, coauthor, and fellow Latino **Robert**. Partnering on this project with you has been a total joy. Our

easy and mutually respectful personal and professional relationship made this an enriching and fun project. Your depth of knowledge, experiences, research rigor, and passion for our subject were assets in themselves. But then came the magic of the synergistic thinking whenever we put our two heads and hearts together. It has been an intellectual- and mission-driven high.

My colleagues at **Korn Ferry**: your smarts, insights, professionalism, collegiality—as well as your passion for better leaders, managers, employees, and corporate cultures—have all made me a better consultant and person.

The **Class of '79** of the American High School of Lima, FDR. Our fusion of Latino, American, Asian, and European vibes taking us through smooth salsa and disco dancing nights after sun-baked beach days of surfing and *ceviche* in our *Lima Querida*, all in the midst of *la dictatura*, the military totalitarianism, were so deeply formative to how I view, understand, and experience the world and my Latino identity. *¡Amigos y amigas de toda la vida!*

And, to my lifelong partner, **Lori**, who, as always, supported yet another project. Hey, *amor, tengo una nueva idea…*

Robert has his own gracias to give to:
Mi amigo Andrés—I've learned so much from you during this collaboration. I'm in awe of your writing style, and I wish to thank you for helping to refine my creative voice. I believe that life is about moments, and I will always treasure our moment of partnership on this endeavor. You and I are proof that friends can work, create, and thrive together. At times, it felt like we were traveling on the same passport. *Un abrazo!*

Our final gracias:

To our interviewees and focus group participants, who gave of their time and energy to share their stories, thoughts, dreams, and aspirations:

Los Angeles Focus Group
Bonizu Ramirez
Erika Maldonado
Ingrid Mendez Janet Perez
Lorena Martínez
Marlene Luna
Natalie Sanchez
Sandra Calles, PhD
Sandra Williams

Dallas Focus Group
Flor Gonzalez
Gabriel Leal
Isaac Padilla
Lisa Rodriguez
Ramir Camu

Chicago Focus Group
Dario Bolanos
Enrique Juarez
Hector Diaz
Isabel Villegas
Marcus Rodriguez
Sofia Curiel
Xiema Duque
Yoly Valencia

New York City Focus Group
Amanda Garcia
Geraldine Cols Azocar
Leonor Ayala
Robert Rivas
Rosemary Martinez
Salvador Mendoza

Mujeres de HACE Focus Group
Barbara Resendiz
Delia McLaughlin
Edith Pacheco
Edna Castro
Faye Aguilar
Karen Saa
Laurin Bello
Marisol Martinez

INDEX

Page numbers in italic indicate figures.

F

faith and religion, and power ambivalence, 182–83

familia (parents, aunts, grandparents), 42–43, 78, 81, 187, 188

family size, and education, 103

family ties, and education, 104

Farías, Jorge, 44–45

feeling, Latino, 11–14

Ferdman, Bernardo, 32, 42, 54–55

Figueredo, Jorge, 46–47, 147–48, 177, 189–90

5% percent shame, xvii, 5, 22, 70, 175–76, 195

Fonsi, Luis, 207

formative years, and leadership style, 161–66

Fraser, George, 185

Freire, Paulo, 175

Fuentes, Carlos, 11, 53

future success

    corporations' role and, 222, 228–31

    described, 10, 225

    government's role and, 227

    Latinas and, 223

    Latinx and, 223

    legacy of Latono executives, 233

    not-for-profits' role and, 228, 231

    universities' role and, 227

G

Galarraga, Juan

    community, 171

    formative years, and leadership style, 165–66

    naysayers, 125

    risk-taking and getting noticed, 131–34

    unapologetic approach, 40–41, 50

Gallegos, Plácida I., 32, 42, 54–55

Galvin, John, 137

Garcia, Charles P., 70–71, 122, 137, 140, 150, 168–69

Garcia, Yvonne, 47–48, 81, 121–22, 123

Gen X

    bicultural identity and, 66, 67, 200, 201

    feeling, Latino, 11

    Latinx generation and, 10

    nationalistic divide and, 54

    research, 2, 198

    sacrifice, power of, 191–92

    survey results, 243–51

Gen Y, xxii

Gen Z, xxii, 66

Glass Ceiling Initiative, 130–31, 160

global impacts, and bicultural identity, 189–91

good enough, dissatisfaction with, 126–27

government, and leadership goals, 10, 176, 183, 227

H

Hace case study, 231–33

HACR (Hispanic Association on Corporate Responsibility), xvii, 5, 22, 171

HACU (Hispanic Association of Colleges and Universities), 100, 101, 183

Hampden-Turner, Charles, 72, 83

Harris Interactive poll in 2013, 5

HBCUs (historically Black colleges and universities), 183

Herrera, George

    identity and I versus we, 82

    nationalistic divide, 55

    opportunities and risk-taking, 134–35

    power ambivalence, 186, 193–94

    relationships, 138–39, 141, 142–43

hierarchy versus egalitarianism, 72, 76–78

Hispanic, as term of use, xxi, xxii–xxiii

Hispanic Association of Colleges and Universities (HACU), xvii, 100, 101, 183

Hispanic Association on Corporate Responsibility (HACR), xvii, 5, 22, 171

Hispanic-serving institutions (HSIs), 101–2, 115, 183, 227

ABOUT THE AUTHORS

Dr. Robert Rodriguez

Robert is the founder and president of DRR Advisors LLC, a diversity consulting firm that specializes in Latino talent initiatives, employee resource group optimization, and diversity strategy.

A leading expert on corporate Latino talent programs, he has worked with over seventy-five corporations including Facebook, NBCUniversal, AT&T, Verizon, Google, Amazon, Walmart, Progressive Insurance, Nike, and State Street Corporation. He previously held leadership roles with the Association of Latino Professionals for America (ALPFA), Target, 3M, RR Donnelley, and the *Washington Post*.

He holds a doctorate in organization development and has taught graduate courses at DePaul University in Chicago and in Latino leadership programs at the University of Southern California (USC) in Los Angeles. He also runs the Latino Leadership Intensive program with Angel Gomez out of Stanford University in Palo Alto and has been a guest lecturer as part of the Latino Leadership Initiative in the Cox School of Business at Southern Methodist University (SMU) in Dallas. He is the author of *Latino Talent: Effective Strategies to Recruit, Retain, and Develop Hispanic Professionals* (Wiley, 2008).

He was named by *Hispanic Business* magazine as one of the top 100 most influential Hispanics in corporate America. He serves on the advisory council for the Hispanic Scholarship Fund and sits on the board of trustees for the National Museum of Mexican Art.

He was born in Lubbock, Texas, the son of Mexican immigrant parents. He has two teenage sons, Bailey and Benjamin, and resides in Chicago with the love of his life, Carmen Sofia Suarez.

Andrés Tomás Tapia

Andrés is senior client partner and the global diversity and inclusion solutions leader at Korn Ferry, a leadership and talent consultancy. He has over twenty-five years of experience as a C-suite management consultant, diversity executive, organizational development and training professional, and journalist.

Prior to Korn Ferry, he was the president of Diversity Best Practices, a diversity and inclusion think-tank and consultancy, and the chief diversity officer and emerging workforce solutions leader for Hewitt Associates. He has worked with dozens of Global 500 organizations such as John Deere, Marriott, United, MassMutual, Allstate, Target, Cigna, HPE, Capital Group, Apple, LinkedIn, and Novartis, as well as non-U.S. multinationals in Brazil, South Korea, and India.

Andrés is the author of *The Inclusion Paradox: The Post-Obama Era and the Transformation of Global Diversity* (Korn Ferry Institute, 2016). He specializes in working with executive teams on developing global enterprise-wide diversity and inclusion strategies while also providing one-on-one executive coaching. He is also a sought-after speaker, the recipient of numerous leadership awards, a trustee with Ravinia Festival, and a board member of the Hispanic Alliance for Career Enhancement (HACE).

Andrés received a bachelor's degree in modern history from Northwestern University with an emphasis in journalism and political science.

He grew up in a bilingual/bicultural home in Lima, Perú. He is married to Lori, a musician. They have one grown daughter, Marisela, who is a professional flamenco dancer.

THE LATINX INSTITUTE

The Latinx Institute is a collaboration between Andrés Tomás Tapia and Dr. Robert Rodriguez that seeks to capture, understand, and synthesize the realities of Latino professionals and leaders in the workplace. Their collaborations include joint public speaking, research, and writing.

Auténtico: The Definitive Guide to Latino Career Success is the first book published by The Latinx Institute.

To contact the authors:
Andrés: *www.inclusionparadox.com*

Robert: *www.drradvisors.com*

Also by Andrés T. Tapia

The 5 Disciplines of Inclusive Leaders
Unleasing the Power of All of Us

In this book, Tapia and Polonskaia draw on Korn Ferry's massive database of 3 million leadership assessments to reveal the essential qualities of inclusive leaders. They discuss the personality traits these leaders share and detail how to develop what they call the five disciplines of inclusive leadership: building interpersonal trust, integrating diverse perspectives, optimizing talent, applying an adaptive mindset, and achieving transformation. Tapia and Polonskaia also identify and bring life to the competencies behind each discipline, describe individual and organizational exemplars of inclusive leadership, and show how the five disciplines enable leaders to unleash the power of all people and to build both structurally and behaviorally inclusive organizations. This book will help leaders foster the skills to deal with today's complex challenges and create a more inclusive, sustainable, and prosperous future for all of us.

Hardcover, ISBN 978-1-5230-8820-1
PDF ebook, ISBN 978-1-5230-8821-8
ePub ebook, ISBN 978-1-5230-8822-5
Digital audio, ISBN 978-1-5230-8823-2

Berrett–Koehler Publishers, Inc.
www.bkconnection.com

800.929.2929

Berrett–Koehler
Publishers

Berrett-Koehler is an independent publisher dedicated to an ambitious mission: *Connecting people and ideas to create a world that works for all.*

Our publications span many formats, including print, digital, audio, and video. We also offer online resources, training, and gatherings. And we will continue expanding our products and services to advance our mission.

We believe that the solutions to the world's problems will come from all of us, working at all levels: in our society, in our organizations, and in our own lives. Our publications and resources offer pathways to creating a more just, equitable, and sustainable society. They help people make their organizations more humane, democratic, diverse, and effective (and we don't think there's any contradiction there). And they guide people in creating positive change in their own lives and aligning their personal practices with their aspirations for a better world.

And we strive to practice what we preach through what we call "The BK Way." At the core of this approach is *stewardship,* a deep sense of responsibility to administer the company for the benefit of all of our stakeholder groups, including authors, customers, employees, investors, service providers, sales partners, and the communities and environment around us. Everything we do is built around stewardship and our other core values of *quality, partnership, inclusion,* and *sustainability.*

This is why Berrett-Koehler is the first book publishing company to be both a B Corporation (a rigorous certification) and a benefit corporation (a for-profit legal status), which together require us to adhere to the highest standards for corporate, social, and environmental performance. And it is why we have instituted many pioneering practices (which you can learn about at www.bkconnection.com), including the Berrett-Koehler Constitution, the Bill of Rights and Responsibilities for BK Authors, and our unique Author Days.

We are grateful to our readers, authors, and other friends who are supporting our mission. We ask you to share with us examples of how BK publications and resources are making a difference in your lives, organizations, and communities at www.bkconnection.com/impact.

Dear reader,

Thank you for picking up this book and welcome to the worldwide BK community! You're joining a special group of people who have come together to create positive change in their lives, organizations, and communities.

What's BK all about?

Our mission is to connect people and ideas to create a world that works for all.

Why? Our communities, organizations, and lives get bogged down by old paradigms of self-interest, exclusion, hierarchy, and privilege. But we believe that can change. That's why we seek the leading experts on these challenges—and share their actionable ideas with you.

A welcome gift

To help you get started, we'd like to offer you a **free copy** of one of our bestselling ebooks:

www.bkconnection.com/welcome

When you claim your **free ebook**, you'll also be subscribed to our blog.

Our freshest insights

Access the best new tools and ideas for leaders at all levels on our blog at ideas.bkconnection.com.

Sincerely,

Your friends at Berrett-Koehler